THE BBC BOOK OF BOWLS

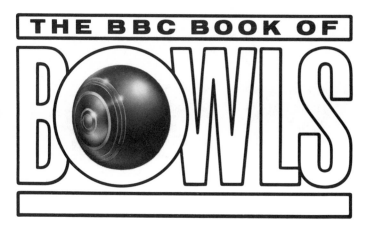

THE BBC BOOK OF BOWLS

COMPILED BY

KEITH PHILLIPS

BBC BOOKS

Published by BBC Books
A division of BBC Enterprises Ltd
Woodlands, 80 Wood Lane, London W12 0TT

First published 1987

© The Contributors and BBC Enterprises Ltd 1987

ISBN 0 563 20587 3

Set in 10/11 pt Sabon
By Phoenix Photosetting, Chatham, Kent
Printed and bound in Great Britain by
Mackays of Chatham Limited

CONTENTS

THE CROWN GAME

INTRODUCTION

The purpose of this book is to entertain, educate and inform the many people who enjoy watching and playing bowls today. It is meant to be light-hearted enough to relax and read at bedtime, but also to be serious enough to read at other times in order to learn something about the sport and to be able to enjoy it. The contributors are well-known to the nation's bowlers and have the expertise and experience to be able to achieve these aims.

I am sure that when you read this book, you will agree that the image bowls used to have as a geriatric pastime should be buried completely. It must now join the ranks as one of the world's top sports, where players need physical endurance, mental strategy and intense concentration to become one of the new superstars of the sport.

The game of bowling has enjoyed a very mixed history, but has progressed substantially since its original conception. Now millions of people, men and ladies, young and old, regularly play the game in both flat and crown green codes. With the advent of indoor bowls clubs this figure has increased substantially, since it enables bowlers to play twelve months of the year. Naturally television, in particular the BBC, has contributed greatly to its more recent popularity and the book gives an insight into the history of televised tournaments, how they are organised and some interesting facts and comments on the players who have taken part. I hope it will provide entertaining reading to all bowlers, as well as to those just interested in the sport by watching on television.

This is not a book which deals comprehensively with any particular type of bowls and there are other books available that deal solely with the finer details of specific types of bowling and techniques. These you could certainly obtain from your local libraries and bookshops for a relatively small expense.

I have received a tremendous amount of encouragement and help from many people in the bowling world in compiling this book, not only from the contributors, but from others as well, whom I am listing overleaf:

Eddie Elson, JP – Retired Secretary of the BCGBA
Jack Leigh – Manager, Waterloo Bowls
Mary Ashcroft – Organiser, Ladies' Waterloo
Fred Rigby – Harry's younger brother
Noel Burrows – Circuit bowler and Manager of *Bowlers*,
Manchester
David Harrison – Managing Director, David Harrison
Promotions, promoter of all indoor television
tournaments.

Finally, I would like to thank my wife Susan for those many hours of typing into the night to produce the original manuscript.

Keith Phillips
April 1987

THE FLAT GAME

CHAPTER 1

A HISTORY OF THE GAME

DAVID RHYS JONES
BBC Bowls Commentator

David Rhys Jones, BBC TV Flat Green commentator

Those viewers who have fallen for the gentle image of the game of bowls had better think again. Of course, it's true that the nods of appreciation, the civilised applause, the polite hand-shakes are genuine enough, but they hide the same aggressive killer-instincts so common – and so obvious – in more violent sports.

Indeed, historically speaking, bowls *was* a violent sport. It took a Scottish lawyer, W. W. Mitchell, to clean up the game a century or so ago. He saw fit to outlaw 'kicking, hacking and tripping' on the sacred turf . . . well, perhaps not so sacred in those days: bowls (like its popular French cousin, boules) was played on any reasonably flat piece of ground, preferably, but not essentially, with a modest covering of grass!

Centuries before Mr Mitchell had civilised the game, bowling alleys were very unsavoury places, 'productive of very evil consequences', and full of 'idle citizens'. They were described as 'the means of promoting a pernicious spirit'. Drinking and gambling were inevitably associated with the game and, like other pub games, bowling was made illegal, chiefly so that the military (young men easily led astray) could actually get on with their archery practice.

Before that, legend has it, when the barbarians were plundering Europe, they found it relaxing after a (successful) battle to set up a game strikingly similar to our bowls. Agreeing on a target object, they would sever the heads of their unhappy opponents and roll them ever so gently across the battle terrain – aiming to get them as close as possible to whatever they chose as a target. Hence, presumably, the expression 'Be up to the head'!

If we travel further back into the mists of time, we find that the Egyptians played marbles with knuckle-bones. This craze for launching a missile at a target seems to be so much a part of human nature that we could claim that bowls was perhaps the second oldest game of them all. Did Adam ever roll an apple at the Tree of Knowledge? I wonder. Certainly every child I know responds to a pebble beach by quite naturally picking up a pebble and throwing it into the sea, often with a target in mind.

Many games have developed from the same roots. Golf, croquet, billiards, snooker, archery and darts all involve targets, but marbles, quoits, skittles, petanque, bocca and bowls all have one thing in common which makes them more primitive and natural games: there is no implement – no club, sling, cue, bat, racket or bow – to distance the man from the ball.

Bowls, like those close cousins, is the simplest of all ball games. If you can roll a ball, you can play bowls. The ball itself is the only artifice . . . after that, it's all hand and eye. Roll the ball in the right direction and at the right speed every time and you'll win every game you play.

But let's get back to the child on the seashore. Maybe he's going for accuracy; maybe, feeling out to impress, he's going for distance. It's clear that shot putting, javelin throwing, caber tossing and even welly whanging have derived from the urge to chuck that pebble out of sight.

In the Middle Ages, strong men would challenge each other to a game of Jactu Lapidum – stone throwing. Much more recently, in 1739, a Croydon farmer placed a bet that he could get from his home to London in 500 throws. He proceeded to complete the eleven-mile journey in 445! Incidentally, some believe that the first syllable of Jactu Lapidum has given bowls the endearing term for the little white target ball – the jack. In some regions the jack is variously referred to as the 'cot', 'kitty', 'pot' or 'white'.

The other projectiles – the larger, black or brown spheroids – are commonly known as woods, again for reasons steeped in history. Woods were once made of wood; lignum vitae (or living wood) is the heaviest timber on this earth. World supplies ran out, and now, as they used to say on *The Goon Show*, 'You can't get the wood'! So today woods are made of plastic, or at least a resin composition: phenol-formaldehyde powder. Rather like bakelite, these plastic woods bear, normally, the commercial name of the manufacturer: hence Henselite, Jacquelite, Phynalite, Vitalite, Drakelite, Tyrolite etc. With all those 'lites', it's surprising the bowls are so heavy – around three and a half pounds each, on average.

Old men still insist that there is nothing quite like the responsive touch of lignum vitae. If you search a bit, you'll see some warped specimens still being trundled – especially in the more remote, rural village clubs. Although still perfectly legal, 'real' woods are not likely to be seen in televised tournaments. Top players, it seems, prefer the greater stability provided by modern chemical technology.

Illustration of a bowling tournament in medieval times

I often receive letters from viewers who criticise me for using the word wood when referring to a bowl. Are you not aware that bowls are now made of composition material, they rather stuffily enquire. I am unrepentant. Woods are part of the rich heritage of sporting vocabulary. Long may the term be used!

There's a story from the days when woods were wooden. I would like to think it is true. A high-society game was being played at Goole in Yorkshire, with Charles Brandon, the Duke of Suffolk, as one of the players. Someone put up a fast one and struck accurately but tragically. One of the Duke's woods cracked and fell into two halves. What was to be done? A sudden brainwave sent Brandon scurrying indoors to the grand hall where the bannister of the impressive staircase terminated in a spherical knob. The protuberance was quickly sawn off and the game continued as though nothing had happened. The Duke, however, soon found that the flattened part of the globe (where it had been attached to the bannister) caused the improvised bowl to run in a curve – a useful device which enabled him to gain access to the jack even when it was hidden behind a forest of short woods. Bias had been invented.

For years bias was imparted by means of weights (brass or pewter) inserted into the bowl, but now (wood or plastic) it's the *shape* of bowl which makes it bend – a quirky quality which prompted Shakespeare to pen this royal exchange in *Richard II*:

Queen: What sport shall we devise here in this garden to
        drive away the heavy thought of care?
Lady: Madam, we'll play at bowls.
Queen: 'Twill make me think the world is full of rubs, and
        that my fortune runs against the bias.

Eleven further references to bowls have been discovered in Shakespeare's plays, although in many cases it is just as likely he was referring to skittles, which was also played in places known as bowling alleys.

Henry VIII (1491–1547) was a devotee of bowls. Although he prohibited his subjects from playing, he installed at Whitehall 'divers fair tennice courts and bowling alleys'. James I (1566–1625) commended 'a moderate practice of bowls' . . . but not by 'the meaner sort of people'! Charles I (1600–1649) was also bowls crazy. He lost a cool thousand at Barking Hall on a green laid by one Richard Shute. It was Charles II (1630–1685) who installed a green at Windsor Castle. It cost him twenty pounds, seven shillings and eleven pence – a sum

which included eight shillings to Will Tonks for four days
work. Enter Cromwell. The Puritans frowned on bowls, as on
so many other enjoyable pastimes, and an era was over.

In spite of all the royal patronage that bowls received, the
most famous historical bowler must be the phlegmatic Sir
Francis Drake. Even Sir Winston Churchill had to agree when
he made one of his historic war broadcasts: 'We must regard
the next week or so as very important weeks in our history.
They rank with the days when the Spanish Armada was
approaching the Channel and Drake was finishing his game of
bowls.'

As one English poet put it:

'He was playing at Plymouth a rubber of bowls
When the great Armada came;
But he said, "They must wait their turn, good souls",
And he stooped and finished the game.'

That picture, cherished by all patriots, was once committed to
canvas by Seymour Lucas. It conjures up true British grit and
sang froid. Sir Francis was indeed a brave nutter.

Engraving after Seymour Lucas. Sir Francis Drake at Plymouth Hoe

It is an interesting sequel to the Drake legend that, although on 19 July 1588 Sir Francis would have been using just two bowls (or woods), there are on display, purporting to be those very woods, one pair at the Sir Francis Drake Bowling Club at Plymouth, one pair at Torquay in Devon, and a single wood at Wellington Bowling Club in New Zealand, and possibly many more 'originals' scattered over the globe.

ASSOCIATION BOWLS

Centuries of feverish and marvellously disorganised activity preceded the civilised game we play today. Man has a fateful way of regulating and institutionalising even the most natural and exuberant activities. Whether or not bowlers wanted it – and at first they certainly didn't – it was inevitable that leagues, associations and federations would develop, and that there should be a call for standardisation and regulation as bowls became first a national and then an international sport.

Skittles became 4-pin, 7-pin, 9-pin or 10-pin, and the modern 10-pin bowling was the ultimate mechanised refinement. Popular in Britain in the Fifties and Sixties, interest seems to have waned, and the all-American sport seems to have made the return trip back across the Atlantic. More resilient, and with deep historic roots, pub skittles is still popular – an integral part of popular culture in many areas, especially in East Anglia and the South West.

Bowls graduated to 'lawn bowling', became respectable and was exported to Australia and other, mainly Commonwealth, countries. There is something very gentlemanly, very *English* about the game, which made it popular with colonials. Another symptom of Man's inclination to impose his will – to regulate nature – was exposed when bowls was first played on rinks, the playing surface confined and defined. Roving jack is the natural game. Stand where you like on the green and deliver the jack wherever you choose. Several other games are going on at the same time, played with similar abandon and territorial freedom. Chaos reigns, but everyone is happy! Well, perhaps not everyone. Someone did decide to regiment the game; to 'fence off' one game from another, and have an orderly, dignified, private game on one's own rink, with no interference and no collisions! That's a feature of the association game.

There were areas of Britain where bowlers held out against the moves to make bowls universal. In the north-west of

England they continued to play on improvised surfaces, and resisted pressure to make greens standard and level. Crown green bowlers have always jealously guarded their independence from mainstream, level green bowls. Indeed they proudly regard themselves as mainstream!

In the north-east of England too, and in East Anglia, they spurned the new up-market image of bowls at the turn of the century, and rejected the association game. Thus developed federation bowls – non-standard greens, no ditches required, a sociable, working-class game emerged, with firm emphasis on drawing to the jack. Firing was forbidden simply because, in many cases, there were no ditches to stop the express bowl's progress into the middle distance and beyond!

Today bowls must be one of the most – if not the very best – organised of all sports. The network of administration required to run the game is so complicated that the unwary fly (sponsor, entrepreneur or media man) who naïvely and hopefully ventures into bowls territory is soon caught in the intricate and sticky spider's web.

Indoor bowls has become popular, women's bowls has strengthened numerically, and each of the four home countries has its own national administration. Consequently, a catalogue of the initials of the ruling bodies inevitably looks like a scrabble board gone berserk.

Outdoors there is the IBB with 10 full and 15 worldwide associate nation members, from America to Zimbabwe, from Zambia to Argentina. The four home countries – EBA, IBA, SBA, WBA – group together as the BIBC, while the ladies are organised by the EWBA, IWBA, SWBA and WWBA. Federation bowls is administered by the EBF and EWBF. Crown green's chiefs are the BCGBA and the BCLCGBA! (British Counties Ladies' Crown Green Bowling Association.)

Indoors there is the EIBA, AIIB, SIBA and WIBA and on the distaff side the EWIBA, IWIBA, SWIBA and WWIBA. They are overseen in the British Isles by the BIIBC and BIWIBC, and one step further, at world level, by the WIBC and WIBCLS. This last body is the World Indoor Bowls Council Ladies' Section – the others I will leave to the reader's fertile imagination (definitely *no* answers on a postcard, *please*!!).

Another indoor variant, and a product of this century, is short mat bowls, strong in Ireland and south Wales, and gaining in popularity in many parts of England. For a brief spell in the late Seventies and early Eighties a 'target' version of the game seemed to be making headway, only to fade away. Even more miniature is the toy game of carpet bowls, which can be played in the average lounge – but not if the affluent home-owner has a shag-pile carpet!

How on earth can the newcomer to bowls hope to sort out this confusing complex of codes, systems and initials? What are the real differences between association, federation and crown? Where are they played? How easy is it to join a club? Can anyone play? The following information is intended to help potential newcomers and might even serve to clarify the issue for confused bowlers.

Firstly, it should be said that IBB/WIBC (association) bowls is the truly international game: the one played outdoors on grass or indoors on carpets, on flat surfaces, and seen on television in such major events as *Jack High*, the World Indoor Singles and Pairs and the UK Championship. It is the game that Mr Mitchell wrote the rules for, the game that Dr W. G. Grace

Dr W. G. Grace, founder of the English Bowling Association

liked so much that he founded the English Bowling Association in 1903, and the game which the general public has come to identify with.

Oddly, no consensus has yet been achieved on whether the game should be called bowls or bowling. Indoors, the association game is run by the World Indoor *Bowls* Council, outdoors by the International *Bowling* Board.

OUTDOOR BOWLS (IBB – ASSOCIATION BOWLS)

At world level, there are, at four-year intervals, World Championships (Aberdeen '84, Auckland '88, Worthing '92) in between the Commonwealth Games contests (Brisbane '82, Edinburgh '86, Auckland '90). England and Australia are the strongest countries numerically, although both Scotland and New Zealand would hotly dispute claims of world domination in terms of achievement. South Africa, too, given the chance, would be very much in the running as a top bowls country, while Canada, USA, Hong Kong, Israel, Ireland and Wales can also muster strong teams.

Although there are minor domestic variations, all countries abide basically by the IBB laws of the game. Greens are square, with sides measuring between 40 and 44 yards. Each rink is between 18 and 19 feet wide, and the green is surrounded by a ditch between two and eight inches deep.

Competitions are arranged for single-handed play (simple head to head), pairs, triples or fours, or for teams. The home

Women's Fours, Sophia Gardens, Cardiff, 1986

international series, for example, requires national teams to put five teams of four on the green. A match between England and Scotland, with 40 keyed-up players crowding the green, is always an intense, competitive and noisy affair. So much for the staid image of the game.

Most bowls, however, is played at club level. Generally the format is team-play, each four in the team comprising lead, second, third and skip. Each player delivers two woods, so there are 16 bowls in the head when each end is complete – a real forest of woods, giving infinite possibilities for pro-motions, take-outs and wicks, and what Richard's Queen called 'rubs'. In triples, generally, even more woods build up – 18 in all or three per player – while in pairs and singles each player as a rule uses four bowls.

Club bowls in England is flourishing. At the last count, in 1986, there were 2683 clubs with 121,630 players affiliated to the English Bowling Association. The figures increase each year, as television introduces bowls to the general public.

Unlike crown and federation, few association clubs are nowadays attached, as in days gone by, to pubs and hostelries. However, whether it's a private or a parks club, the social side of bowls is still of vital importance. Most clubs have a clubhouse with bar, where the 22nd end is the equivalent of golf's 19th hole – the place for post-mortems over a pint.

The EBA championships are held every year at Beach House Park in Worthing – also the venue for the televised *Jack High* series covered in detail elsewhere in these pages. Not sur-prisingly, David Bryant is England's most prolific cham-pionship winner, having bagged an extraordinary 16 titles since 1957.

Wynne Richards has been the English champion two years out of three, while Chris Ward is another recent double winner. John Bell, Andy Thomson and David Cutler are also recent champions, while it will surprise many that at the time of writing Tony Allcock has yet to win his first EBA title in any of the four main events – singles, pairs, triples and fours – although he won the Junior singles a record three times.

Thirty-five counties are affiliated to the EBA, ranging in size from lowly Lancashire, with eight clubs, to Surrey with 213. The only English counties without flat green EBA bowls are Cheshire, Shropshire and Staffordshire, which are firmly en-trenched in the crown green code.

David Bryant – in action

Any enquiries about the English Bowling Association or any of its clubs or counties should be directed to the EBA Secretary, David Johnson, at 2a Iddesleigh Road, Bournemouth, BH3 7JR, telephone (0202) 22233.

INDOOR BOWLS (WIBC – ASSOCIATION BOWLS)

Indoor bowls began almost one hundred years ago as a make-shift winter substitute for the summer lawn game. It is a substitute no longer. Whether traditionalists like it or not, the gentle click of lignum vitae on the village green is being replaced by the competitive cut-and-thrust of plastic woods on carpets of man-made fibre.

Scotsman William Macrae girded his bowls with rubber bands and experimented on a sawdust-covered concrete floor in Drumdryan Drill Hall in 1888. Years later, Edinburgh folk bowled by gaslight in the cellars of the Synod Hall while the ubiquitous bearded cricketing Doctor was influential in founding an indoor club at Crystal Palace in 1906.

Today indoor bowls is booming. In place of the finely manicured lawns, the game is played in great stadiums, on carpets – green in hue, 40 yards square and as smooth as the best snooker tables. There are now over 200 indoor clubs in England, 32 in Scotland, 10 in Wales and four in Ireland, all busily occupied morning, afternoon and evening with local leagues, friendlies and national competitions. They offer a great social service to the community, and a good deal more. Sponsors have recognised the business potential of indoor bowls, and a game which started as a Cinderella 'section' of the outdoor game has become the guest of honour at the Ball.

Embassy have been connected with the World Indoor Singles since 1979. CIS have sponsored the UK Singles since 1983, and were generous bowls benefactors before that. Midland Bank joined in in 1986, sponsoring the first World Indoor Pairs Championship at Bournemouth. The listening bank had evidently heard some good things about indoor bowls!

Rules are virtually the same as outdoors. It *is*, some say, the same game. Certainly a good player on grass is also a good player on carpet, and vice versa – as a rule. But like all rules, there are exceptions, and while bowlers like Willie Wood, Chris Ward, Jimmy Hobday and David Cutler seem to prefer the great outdoors, others, like Terry Sullivan, Jim Baker, David Corkill, Roy Cutts and, to some extent, Tony Allcock, perform more happily with a roof over their heads.

As yet, indoor bowls is very much a British preserve. Our climate, I suppose, prompted us to pioneer. Our summer season is so short and so unreliable that a move indoors was always an attractive proposition. Most top players, however, much as they like playing in the open air with the sun on their

Willie Wood, Scotland's ace outdoor international

backs, now state a preference for the relatively stable, true, predictable conditions indoors.

Although their climate is kinder, Australia and New Zealand now have indoor stadiums – that at Tweed Heads in Melbourne is said to be the finest in the world. Both nations have been admitted to the World Indoor Bowls Council. There is at least one modest facility in the States, and a couple in Canada, where conditions seem ideal for a boom in indoor bowls over the next few years.

Any enquiries about the English Indoor Bowling Association or any of its clubs should be directed to the EIBA Secretary, Bernard Telfer, at 290a Barking Road, London, E6 3BA, telephone (01) 470 1237.

OUTDOOR BOWLS (EBF – FEDERATION BOWLS)

The English Bowling Federation was founded in 1926, but has origins dating much further back. Now played in 13 English counties from Northumberland to Essex, federation bowls may be less sophisticated than its EBA counterpart, but it is just as vigorous in its own way.

There are so few differences between EBF and EBA that many may ask why the Federation hold on to their independence. The justification for the existence of the EBF is really an historic one, but there are features of federation bowls which are distinct and attractive today.

Federation bowlers normally bowl with two woods, in team games as well as singles. They do not play fours, and tend to call their basic two-wood triples game 'rinks'. They do not insist that their surfaces conform to such strict standards as their EBA rivals, and they are more tolerant to the concept of mixed bowling – indeed they encourage it. There is a warm, friendly atmosphere to their game.

An emphasis on drawing to the jack, already explained, is encouraged by the ruling 'no bowl shall count which lays more than six feet from the jack'. There are no 'touchers'. Federation bowlers are understandably proud of their drawing ability.

Clearly the existence of sometimes substandard greens in country districts gives welcome opportunities for competition to many. Two-wood play means quicker games – a boon for working men and women with limited leisure time, and useful during our shorter evenings.

Championship finals are held at Skegness every August when, of course, the winners have no prospect of going further. Federation bowls is confined to England so there are no British championships or international events, and in order to gain international recognition, top federation bowlers often join EBA clubs to further their ambitions. Chris and David Ward, Roy Cutts and John Ottaway are among today's top stars who were brought up on the EBF game.

Any enquiries about the English Bowling Federation or any of its clubs or counties should be directed to the EBF Secretary, John Webb, at 62 Frampton Place, Boston, Lincs., PE21 8EL, telephone (0205) 66201.

OUTDOOR BOWLS (CROWN GREEN)

The roving jack principle of crown green bowls firmly places it as, probably, the most genuine and natural form of bowls. Many greens are still attached to hostelries, and there is a robust, down-to-earth quality to the game, as well as a sense of real professionalism which has only recently become evident in the level green game.

Crown green tournaments were popular on television long before the current growth of the top flat events had been envisaged and spectator participation has always been a feature of crown.

In my opinion there are three factors which have blunted the appeal of the crown. Firstly, it is such a *difficult* game that the jack is not often threatened with suffocation. Secondly, the basic two-wood game limits tactical options in the head. Thirdly, geographical limitations mean that (although Wales can field a fair team from its north-coast greens) crown green bowls is not truly an international game in the sense that level green bowls clearly is.

Crown green bowlers share many skills with their flat green counterparts, but the strategy of the two codes is quite different. Indeed, crown green bowls is such a unique, independent game that it earns a full chapter in its own right (see page 83).

The men's game is administered by the British Crown Green Bowling Association (BCGBA), and the women's side of the game is at last becoming formalised as the British Counties Ladies' Crown Green Bowling Association (BCLCGBA).

Any enquiries about crown green bowls should be directed to the Secretary of the BCGBA, R. Holt, 14 Leighton Avenue, Maghull, Liverpool, L31 0AH; telephone (051) 5268367.

INDOOR BOWLS (SHORT MAT)

Rain stopped play. A familiar sporting scourge sent two teams of Belfast bowlers seeking shelter in a church hall. The hall was carpeted. 'Why not . . .?' thought the enterprising Irish – and the short mat game was born in 1926! Now there are 900 clubs in Ireland, catholic *and* protestant, north *and* south of the border, with over 40,000 estimated members. This seemingly makeshift game is dynamically and numerically more vigorous than the orthodox game – which in 1987 could boast only four stadiums in the whole of Ireland!

A similar thing happened in Wales. Bowls fanatics in the Rhondda moved indoors in the winter so that they could play their favourite summer game for 12 months of the year. They, too, rolled out mats in church halls and working men's clubs and formed the WIBA in 1934.

At first, the mats were all shapes and sizes, but gradually some order was imposed to regulate a booming pastime. The IIBA was formed in 1961, and the short mat people *still* use the initials, jealously denying them to the 'proper', full-size green national body.

While the Welsh went all respectable (a full-size stadium in Cardiff with a hyperbolic paraboloid roof) or played an ad hoc hybrid game (there are only about 20 *genuine* short mat clubs in Wales) the Irish game grew and grew – and eventually crossed the Irish Sea. There are around 15 short mat clubs in the Stranraer area in Scotland, and the English Short Mat Bowling Association, formed in Stockport in 1984, now has almost 300 affiliated clubs.

Mats are between 40 and 50 feet long and only 6 feet wide. Although full-size bowls are used, there are cross-boards to minimise firing, and, of course, no ditches. While some might dismiss it as a toy game, there is certainly great interest and lively competition – and no participant *ever* thinks of short mat as a second-rate substitute for the real thing!

A total 2800 enter the Irish short mat singles championship – and there are pairs, triples and fours events as well. Finals are played in the Antrim Forum.

Rod McCutcheon and Margaret Johnston, two famous Irish internationalists at the 'grown-up' game, also play keenly on short mats. To universal delight, Rod, himself only 24, was recently beaten in a big short mat event – by a 12-year-old boy. The lad added injury to insult by asking for McCutcheon's autograph at the end of the game.

Short mat is clearly a fine game in its own right, and has now taken such a foothold in all four home countries that a home international series was held at Blackpool in 1986, with the 1987 series taking place in Coleraine, Northern Ireland.

Any enquiries about the short mat game in Ireland – its true home – should be directed to the Secretary of the Irish Indoor Bowling Association, Ronnie McDermott, telephone (0232) 794869.

CHAPTER 2

HOW TO PLAY

JIMMY DAVIDSON
Director of Coaching, English Bowls Coaching Scheme

Jimmy Davidson, now established in the BBC TV commentary team

IT'S EASY TO LEARN

Bowls is a simple game, based on a fairly natural physical movement. It's easy to learn, and there are plenty of qualified instructors willing to teach absolute beginners. It invariably pleases and surprises new learners that within a couple of hours of beginning their instruction, they can take part in a competitive game of bowls.

It has always been the case that any man, woman, boy or girl calling in at their local bowls club would find a member who would help them to learn to play. These days, in England alone, there are nearly 3000 Certificated Instructors. They teach in accordance with the syllabus and guidelines of the English Bowls Coaching Scheme. The instruction they give is practical, on the green, without any prior verbal discourse.

The object of the game is to get your bowl(s) nearer to the jack than your opponent. The jack is the spherical white 'target' object, less than 1lb in weight and about 2½ inches in diameter. The jack is delivered first up to a maximum distance of 40 yards and a minimum of 25 yards. The first jack is delivered by the player(s) who wins the toss; thereafter the winner of each game or 'end' bowls the jack first.

In the flat game, there are four different types of match: 1) Singles 2) Pairs 3) Triples 4) Fours. The scoring in each match is the same; the nearest bowl(s) to the jack takes the point.

Singles   Each player has four bowls and can therefore score up to four points an end. Normally, the first to score 21 points wins. Currently, in televised tournaments indoors, the players have to win a given number of 'sets'. A set is won by the first player to reach seven points.

Pairs   Two players per team. Each player has four bowls and the first to 21 points wins. In some TV Indoor Tournaments, there are two-bowl pairs, ie each player has two bowls and in this format, the winners have to beat their opponents in a given number of sets, each set consisting of seven ends.

Triples   Three players per team. Each player has three bowls and the first team to reach 18 points wins.

Fours   Four players per team. Each player has two bowls and the first team to reach 21 points wins.

In the crown green game each player always has two bowls and the scoring system is the same: ie nearest bowl(s) to the jack wins. There are usually three different maximum points targets per match. Most games are played 21 up or 31 up, with some pairs competitions even going to 41 up.

EQUIPMENT AND BOWL SELECTION

The learner, who should dress in casual clothes, will be equipped with a pair of flat-soled shoes, or overshoes, and lent a set of four bowls to use.

There are eight different sizes of bowl, varying in diameter from 4⅝ inches to 5⅛ inches, and varying in weight to a maximum of 3lb 8oz each. Each bowl of the set of four is identical, and all 'turn' the same amount on the same green. That is to say that the 'bias' of the four bowls has been precisely matched in manufacture.

The bias of different sets can vary. The rule is that every bowl must 'bend' more than a master bowl kept in each country. Instructors advise each beginner not to buy a set of bowls until they learn how to play, and have found out which make, weight and size suits them best.

A set of bowls will last a bowling lifetime. Costs vary, but the average cost is of the order of about £80 for the set, representing the major part of the total cost of preparing to play the game, socially or competitively.

DELIVERY ACTION

It is a fundamental principle of the English Bowls Coaching Scheme that every bowler's delivery action is as unique as their fingerprints. Although several actions can be categorised by a general description (eg Crouch, Athletic etc) each action is different, in some detailed respect, from every other action.

A further principle of the Scheme is that, to be acceptable, the adopted action of any beginner needs to satisfy only three criteria:

a   That it is comfortable, ie it does not produce unnecessary strain and can be precisely repeated for long periods of play.

b   That it is effective – it will not be measured by theoretical imperatives related to its constituent parts.

c   That it conforms with the laws of the game, ie that the whole of one foot is on, or directly above, the confines (24″ × 14″) of the bowls mat at the precise moment the bowl leaves the hand.

Until recently, the method of instruction used to establish the delivery action which suited each beginner was to get the learner to copy demonstrations of several different types of action. The instructor and pupil then chose the action which seemed to be producing the best results.

This method of starting the instruction process was changed fairly recently in England. Now the beginner is invited to stand on the bowls mat and given a jack. He, or she, is then asked to roll the jack to the instructor, positioned some seven to ten yards away.

Their natural movement in rolling what is, to every one of them, a fairly familiar object to handle – a ball about the same size as a tennis ball – is what the instructor uses in helping the learner to groove in a bowls delivery action.

Repeated rolling of the jack, over increased distances, is used by the instructor to build on that which is inherent and good, and to eliminate that which, if uncorrected, might produce error. Good stance, timing and rhythm can already be present, or produced by encouraging correction, in this repetition.

The instructor then varies the places where he stands, in relation to the mat, so that the learner has to vary his stance on the mat, changing the position of his feet to accommodate the new angles of delivery from the mat. Once an acceptable delivery action has been established using the jack, the beginner is then ready to repeat the action using a bowl. This is the point at which the instructor explains:

a Bias
b Forehand and Backhand
c Line and Length

BIAS

It is the shape of a bowl which makes it turn. (Many people believe, in error, that one side of the bowl is more heavily weighted than the other.) As the bowl slows down, the surface on which the bowl runs turns towards the side on which the disc is the smaller.

The diagram on page 33 shows the forehand path of a bowl to a short jack, and a full-length jack. It can be seen that the first part of the route travelled to both lengths is the same. It is only at the point when the bowl loses impetus and begins to travel much more slowly that it begins to turn. This point is known as the 'shoulder' for that length of jack. It is usually about two-thirds of the distance towards the point at which the bowl will come to rest.

It will also be seen that the direction in which the bowl must be aimed is the same for the two different lengths of jack. This is known as the line on that hand or that rink (number two in this case) of that green.

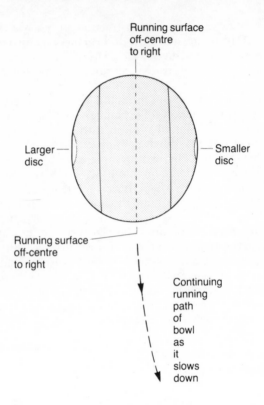

Running surface
off-centre
to right

Larger — disc

Smaller disc

Running surface off-centre to right

Continuing running path of bowl as it slows down

FOREHAND AND BACKHAND

The side of the rink on which the bowl is shown to be travelling in the diagram is the forehand. If the bowl was played on the other side of the rink it would be on the backhand.

In bowls, the terms forehand and backhand are the same as for the racquet sports. A right-handed player, playing on his right-hand side as he looked at the jack, would be playing on that forehand. On the left-hand side, it would be his backhand.

The small disc side of the bowl, ie the bias side, is always on the inside of the curve towards the jack.

LINE AND LENGTH

A bowl delivered in the correct direction, which finishes on the centre line of the rink, has been bowled on the right line.

A bowl delivered with the correct amount of impetus, or

weight, so that it finishes at the same distance from the mat as the jack, has been bowled with the right length.

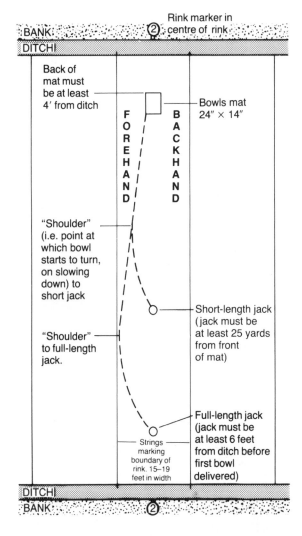

A bowl delivered on the right line with the right length is a perfectly-played bowl – it *is* a simple game. If he gets just two things right with every bowl, then a bowler will be playing perfect bowls. But no bowler will ever achieve perfection.

DELIVERY ACTIONS – SOME FAMOUS EXAMPLES

The most commonly-used bowls action is the athletic, or upright, action, but individual actions can vary to a considerable degree, and still all be described as athletic or upright.

The three pictures below show the finish of a typical Australian delivery action. Ken Williams, who played in the World Indoor Singles in 1985 and 1986, has as good a record of bowling achievements as any current Australian bowler.

You'll see from these pictures that the whole body is moving in perfect co-ordination, with movement of left leg and bowling arm finishing at the same split second.

Ken Williams – Delivery action

Look at the next three pictures below, showing the finish of the delivery action of Peter Belliss, the current World Outdoor Singles Champion. In his case it can be seen that the arm action continues long after the first foot has stopped.

Peter hails from New Zealand, where the bowling greens need less weight, or impetus, on the bowl than anywhere else in the world. Because the only body movement in the latter part of the action is of the bowling arm, the required lesser impetus comes solely from arm movement, and does not include impetus which would stem from transfer of body weight to the front foot.

Peter Belliss – Delivery action

One bowler became a World Champion partly because he watched a BBC television transmission of a bowls event. One of the bowlers who took part, with success, in the *Jack High* programmes of the Kodak Masters from Worthing in the early 1980s was Bill Moseley from South Africa.

Bill Moseley uses the South African 'clinic' style of delivery. This style was pioneered by Dr Julios Seigay of Johannesburg. He worked with what he termed a clinic of twelve top South African bowlers in 1961 to produce an action with very limited body movement. The theory is that if there is little body

Terry Sullivan – Delivery action

movement, there is less to go wrong in the action (rather like cricketers cutting out backswing of the bat by standing with the bat already taken back).

Terry Sullivan of Wales watched Bill Moseley playing on BBC-TV, and, after some 30 years as a bowler, decided to change his action to the South African clinic style. The next four pictures show Terry winning the 1985 World Indoor Singles Championship, televised by the BBC from Coatbridge, Scotland, in February of that year.

Somewhat ironically, the bowler Terry beat in the 1985 final was South African-born Cecil Bransky of Israel, who also uses the clinic style.

Whenever a new bowler has difficulty with co-ordination of body movement, I recommend the clinic style.

With slight variations from the basic style, the five bowlers who won all the five gold medals in Singles, Pairs, Triples, Fours and Team in the 1976 World Outdoor Championships for South Africa used the clinic style. The five were Doug Watson, Bill Moseley, Nando Gatti, Kelvin Campbell and Kel Lightfoot. The reserve for the team was Cecil Bransky.

THE SHOTS IN THE GAME

The main basic shots played in bowls are:

a The Draw Shot
b Resting Shot
c Resting-out Shot
d The Jack Trail
e Using a Bowl
f Follow-through, or Follow-on, Shot
g Fire, or Drive
h Block, or Stopper
i Position Bowl

THE DRAW SHOT

The draw shot is the first shot to learn, and the shot most used in bowls. The dotted lines in the diagram opposite show the drawing line which might be required on the forehand, and backhand, of a rink.

In the use of the forehand, the line required is outside a bowl already played, and in the use of the backhand, inside a bowl already played. X marks the spots where it is intended the bowl will finish.

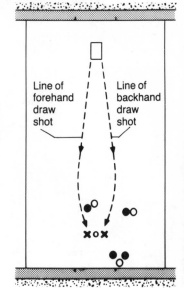

Line of forehand draw shot

Line of backhand draw shot

Key

o   Jack

O   Bowls of bowler to play next — white

●   Opposing bowls — black

✗   Intended finishing position of bowl.

RESTING SHOT

The resting shot is played when another bowl, already played, is available to use as a drawing target. The diagram opposite shows a position where a resting shot might be played.

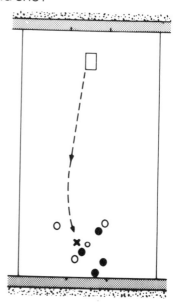

RESTING-OUT SHOT

The resting-out shot differs from the resting shot in that it is played with sufficient impetus to knock an opposing bowl some distance away from the jack. The diagram opposite shows a position where a resting-out shot would be attempted.

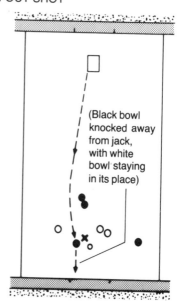

(Black bowl knocked away from jack, with white bowl staying in its place)

THE JACK TRAIL

The diagram opposite shows a good opportunity for 'white' to trail the jack to his own three waiting bowls.

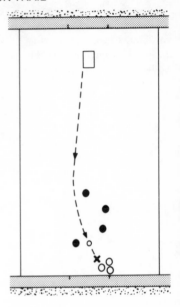

USING A BOWL

In the diagram opposite, the 'white' player might try to 'use' one of his own bowls because both forehand and backhand are blocked for the draw shot, in that opposing bowls are on the path a draw shot would follow.

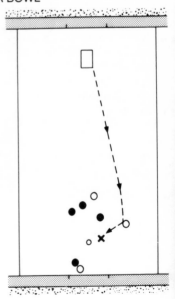

FOLLOW-THROUGH, OR FOLLOW-ON, SHOT

In the position facing 'white' opposite, he might decide to play a follow-through, or follow-on, shot. He would be aiming to contact one of the opposing bowls with sufficient force to retain sufficient impetus to follow-through and finish close to the jack, but not so much weight that he travels too far past the jack.

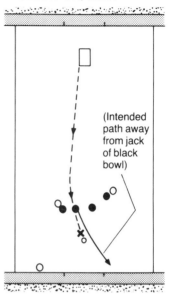

(Intended path away from jack of black bowl)

FIRE, OR DRIVE

The position illustrated opposite would call for a drive or fire by 'white'. The bowl is played with the maximum impetus the player can impart to the bowl without losing control of accuracy of line.

The prime target is the jack to be forced through to the waiting bowls, but if slightly off the required line, the drive would remove opposing scoring bowls.

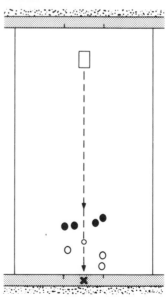

BLOCK, OR STOPPER

A block, or stopper, is played to prevent the opponent from playing on a specific route or line with his next bowl. In the diagram opposite 'white' is attempting to stop on the line his opponent would take if he were to drive. X marks the spot where 'white' is trying to place his bowl.

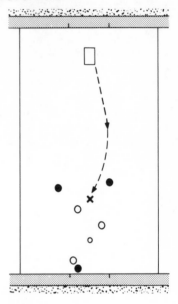

POSITION BOWL

A position bowl is played to reduce the scoring possibilities for the opponent. In the diagram opposite, 'white' is attempting to finish in position X to stop his opponent scoring four shots with a jack-trailing shot on the forehand.

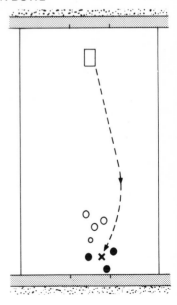

CHAPTER 3

THE FLAT GAME ON TELEVISION

OUTDOOR

JACK HIGH

JOHNNIE WATHERSTON
BBC Sports Producer

1987, believe it or not, is the tenth anniversary of *Jack High* and over those years the BBC has introduced bowls to millions of people who previously hadn't appreciated what a wonderfully skilful and exciting game it could be.

In many respects, *Jack High* has done for flat green bowls what *Pot Black* did for snooker. Over the years our audiences have steadily grown with the game really taking off now as a television sport. Thousands of pounds in prize money are available and more and more young people are taking up the game.

The obvious difference between *Jack High* and the other televised tournaments is that it is played outdoors. This to the non-player may not appear to make much difference. After all the objective is still the same: get your bowls nearer the jack than your opponents. But on the greens at Worthing there is a totally different atmosphere to that of Coatbridge or Preston. The clouds scud across the Downs, the sun shines most of the time, and the crowds relax in their deckchairs around the green.

The weather gives the players much to consider. The rink speeds up or slows down, depending on which direction the wind is blowing, and what the variations on the rink are from one end to the other. Carpets, on the other hand, are uniform. They don't change pace and don't need cutting every morning. We also have some unscheduled intervals at Beach House Park, Worthing – a cat runs across the green with its lunch in its mouth, a squirrel darts out for a tasty morsel and the pigeons and sparrows descend to pick up grass seeds. All very distracting for the players, but part of the established scene which has helped *Jack High* grow the way it has over the years.

When I first went down to Beach House Park in 1978 the only bowls that had been televised from there were the World Championships in 1972. In fact bowls had hardly been on

Beach House Park, Worthing, during *Jack High*

television at all. For the World Championships a vast cross-shaped scaffolding had been built to allow camera access to all four greens. *Jack High* was totally different, an event staged specifically for television, intimate and confined to one green, so I had to start from scratch.

We had four cameras available and it seemed that the best way to cover this sport, of which I had no previous experience, was head on, so that the viewers could see the curve of the bowl as it headed for the jack. Then they must be able to see from above the relative distances between bowls and jack so at a glance they could tell who was lying shot. Being outdoors, though, there is no roof on which to hang an overhead camera, so we had to compromise by building a high scaffolding at one end of the green to accommodate the commentary box and one camera, with a second camera elevated at the other end. More recently, we have introduced a hand-held camera which roves around the green getting pictures from different angles. Woe betide anybody who falls asleep in the sun at the side of the green! All the camera positions we decided upon in 1978 have in fact hardly changed. Now we were ready to fulfil the brief of making seven half-hour programmes for BBC-2. They were to be transmitted on consecutive nights, which again was an experiment for television.

The format of *Jack High* is that eight of the leading players in the world are invited to compete; they are then divided into two groups of four, playing each other on a 'round robin' basis with the top two players from each group going through to the semi-finals.

The players are naturally the most important ingredient in *Jack High*, and what players we have had over those years: World Champions, Commonwealth Champions and National Champions. From all corners of the globe they have come – Australia, New Zealand, Fiji, Hong Kong, the USA, Canada, South Africa, Israel, Ireland and Great Britain. Perhaps the most famous of them all is David Bryant, who over the years has kept an amazing record of consistency.

The commentary team that first year was David Vine, still very much with us and who I know looks forward to his trip to Worthing each year, and the late Graham Howard. Graham was a delightful man with a wicked sense of humour, who I am sure would be the first to admit he found the complexities of television most perplexing. He subsequently became one of the markers for the series and added greatly to the proceedings in his own inimitable way. David Rhys Jones joined the team in 1979. He is an international bowler in his own right, so he knows what he is talking about.

On the Thursday morning our vehicles arrive at Beach House Park, the cables are installed for the cameras and hopefully by about four o'clock in the afternoon all is working and ready.

The first match starts at 9.30 am on the Friday morning and we record everything that moves, bearing in mind that all the 'round robin' matches are theoretically important. The two Davids commentate as it happens and as the groups unfold we get more selective and only concentrate on the matches which are relevant to decide which two players from each group will proceed to the semi-finals. On the Sunday we again record all of the two semi-final matches and then the final. By the time the winner receives his trophy we have miles and miles of videotape from which to select the best matches, best ends and even best shots for our seven programmes.

When the players and officials sit down to their end of tournament dinner, we meet in our hotel and work out the exact content of each programme, because the next morning David Vine has to record all the little bits and pieces that bind the whole thing together. We have detailed notes on everything that has been recorded, which tell us how long a certain end took, how good it was, the scores and anything unusual that has happened. From this the story of the tournament evolves and we leave David Vine at about one in the morning to get on with it. I'm not sure what he does between then and ten o'clock the next morning, but he reappears at Beach House Park on the Monday morning with all his introductions and links written. He then proceeds to deliver them all to camera straight off, the odd pause to check detail and then off again. It is a great feat and by lunchtime we have all the material necessary to make the new series of *Jack High*. A few weeks later all the segments are artistically welded together in the videotape department in the basement of Television Centre.

The programme is a team effort, both from the BBC's point of view and from the tournament's. Worthing make sure all is spick and span around the greens with always a lovely floral display. The greens have been tended lovingly over the years by Jock Munro, who always has an inexhaustible supply of stories.

THE STORY SO FAR, OR 'JACK HIGHLIGHTS'

1978   The 75th anniversary of the English Bowling Association and David Bryant heads the list of eight international bowlers, including Bill Moseley (South Africa), David McGill (Scotland) and Dick Folkins (USA).

This year saw the controversial firing shot make its television debut. Dick Folkins, a veteran highway engineer from California, outdrew David Bryant in the final, only to see his cosy clusters smashed off the green by the belligerent Bryant, who won all his matches and beat Folkins 21–12 in the final.

The television audience started at half a million and grew to two million, an encouraging start.

1979   Two new players from the Antipodes – Phil Skoglund from New Zealand and Barry Salter of Australia.

Folkins shone again, gaining sweet revenge against Bryant in the very first game of the competition. Bryant recovered, and went on to the semi-final. Willie Murray's Irish antics entertained the large crowds, though there were a few rude words from the director as Willie danced out of shot, or stood between camera and the head!

The series was increased from seven to eight programmes because of a brilliant semi-final between Bryant and Bill Moseley of South Africa, which demanded two programmes. Bryant won the match 21–18 and three and a half million watched.

Bryant won his second consecutive title against the cheeky little Scotsman David McGill 21–11.

1980 Again increased to eight programmes, with David Bryant losing his chance of three successive titles to David McGill. At one stage Bryant led 18–13, but McGill went on to win the semi 21–19. McGill, an Edinburgh architect, has recently become better known for his talking than for his bowling. He's part of the BBC's regular commentary team. Athletic Aussie Barry Salter reached his second successive semi-final. The New Zealand representative was Kerry Clark (the next President of the International Bowling Board). In another good final, McGill lost to Bill Moseley 21–16.

1981 Doug Watson of South Africa, the 1976 World Champion, came to Worthing in 1981, as did Peter Belliss of New Zealand, who gave an exhibition of the most lethal firing.

McGill again beat Bryant, 21–16, but lost again to Moseley, 21–14, in a repeat of the 1980 final. It was the chirpy Scot's third silver medal in three years! The game between 1980 World Champion, David Bryant, and 1976 World Champion Doug Watson was of special interest. As a South African, Watson had been unable to defend his World title at Frankston in 1980, when Bryant had regained it. Bryant beat Watson, 21–15.

1982 A new face from Australia this year, John Snell. He was silver medallist in both the Commonwealth Games 1978 and the World Championships in 1980 and proved his expertise by reaching the final at his first attempt. David Bryant scraped into the semis on shot difference, having lost to Peter Belliss 21–16 and Cecil Bransky 21–20 in the 'round robin' section. But being the competitor that he is, he won the final 21–12 to take his third *Jack High* title in five years. Moseley, a popular winner for two years, went down 11–21 to Bryant in the semi-final. Bryant's final victory over Snell involved a characteristic Clevedon come-back.

1983 A new country and a new face for *Jack High*, George Souza from Hong Kong – plus the 1982 Commonwealth gold medallist, Willie Wood. In the first match of the tournament Souza beat David Bryant 21–18 and it wasn't a flash in the pan because they met again in the final, and what an extraordinary affair *that* was. They were locked together at 18–18 when the heavens opened; not rain, but hail! After Jock Munro had squeegeed the green they resumed, Souza just winning 21–19.

1984 Two Souzas in 1984! George, from Hong Kong, was joined by Frank, from California, but claimed no kinship. Could either Souza march through the very first Gateway? Not while Bryant and Belliss were playing so well! Peter Belliss, a former Wanganui lock-forward whose grandfather Moke skippered the All Blacks, actually went on to win the World singles title at Aberdeen a few weeks later, but he couldn't stop Bryant winning his fourth *Jack High* tournament, 21–16.

1985 Joker John Bell, a Carlisle planning officer, and another member of the BBC bowls commentary team, also made his *Jack High* bid in 1985. He played well enough, but tragically let the holder (Bryant) off the hook in his first game.

Another Canadian proved popular – and successful. Liverpool-born Ron Jones, a 5ft 2in featherweight is, unbelievably, a sheet-metal worker. Sporting his natty jockey-cap, he lost the 3rd/4th play-off to John Bell. Bryant became *Jack High* champion for the fifth time, beating Tel Aviv sweet-shop owner Cecil Bransky 21–12 in the final.

1986 That man Bryant again, but also two new exciting players from Down Under: Rob Parrella from Australia – another mean firer – and Ian Dickison from New Zealand, who reached the final at his first attempt. He defeated Bryant in the early round 21–18, but the Master had the last laugh, winning probably the best final yet 21–19 – his sixth title out of nine played since it all started in 1978. Ian Dickison went on to win the singles gold medal at the Commonwealth Games in Edinburgh two months later.

WORLD CHAMPIONSHIPS AND COMMONWEALTH GAMES

DAVID RHYS JONES

Bowls was played in the first British Empire Games (as the Commonwealth Games were originally known) in Hamilton, Ontario, in 1930. Since then, bowls has been an important feature of every Games – apart from 1966, in Jamaica, where there are sadly no bowling greens.

In 1966, to make up for the absence of bowls from the Games line-up, the first World Bowls championships were held

– in Kyeemagh, Sydney, Australia. The second championships took place at Worthing six years later, in 1972, since when World Bowls has been celebrated regularly at four-yearly intervals: Johannesburg in 1976, Melbourne in 1980, Aberdeen in 1984. Auckland hosts World Bowls in 1988, while Worthing is already preparing for a triumphant return of the championships to the famous Beach House Park greens in 1992.

BBC-TV cameras were at Worthing in 1972 to capture the remarkable antics of the extrovert Scot, Harry Reston, who was famous for his loud verbal exhortations to his bowls and to himself. 'You're well-played, Harry!' was his favourite cry of self-acclaim!

Although Harry and his Scottish team-mates were not quite well-played enough to win any of the four events, they won the team accolade – the Leonard Trophy – for the best overall performance.

Bowls, of course, was not an established TV sport in those days. By all accounts, a particular editor of *Grandstand*, noticeably without any particular affection for bowls, was heard to say, 'Stand by . . . We're coming to the bowls . . . and let's 'ave some more of that noisy little bugger!' Perhaps it was the irresistibly ostentatious behaviour of Harry Reston in 1972 that sowed the seeds of bowls on TV?

By the time World Bowls arrived at Aberdeen in 1984, the general public were beginning to recognise the likes of Peter Belliss, Tony Allcock, Jim Baker, Willie Wood and, of course, David Bryant. BBC Scotland covered the event, and beamed the pictures nationwide.

John Bell (now a commentator himself and a contributor to this publication) was Tony Allcock's lieutenant in winning the fours for England, supported by George Turley and Julian Haines. All four appeared in kilts in a final ceremony which brought the house down.

Jim Baker for Ireland skipped Stan Espie (a natural comedian) and Sammy Allen to the triples title, while the pairs contest produced a Scottish gold medallist – representing the USA! Young George Adrain from Dreghorn came in as a substitute for American Jimmy Candelet (injured leg) and led superbly for Skippy Arculli. The makeshift pair beat Bryant and Allcock in the final.

The highlight of the event, without doubt, was the singles final. Peter Belliss of New Zealand scored a narrow victory over Willie Wood from Scotland in the final end, and won 21–20.

Scotland took the Leonard team trophy without actually winning an event. Shades of Worthing in 1972! There was heavy rain at Aberdeen, flooding the Westburn Park greens during the first week of the competition.

There was also heavy rain two years later at Edinburgh during the Commonwealth Games. The heavens opened, and within four minutes the Balgreen complex – greens and all – was underwater! When the flood subsided, another determined Kiwi, Ian Dickison, proceeded to strike gold. Ian beat rugged Aussie Ian Schuback and Edinburgh postman Richard Corsie (then only 19) into silver and bronze medal positions.

George Adrain (with his consistent lead, Grant Knox) won the men's pairs – this time for his own Scotland! Wendy Line of England thoroughly deserved her ladies' singles gold medal, while Ireland's immaculate Margaret Johnston (supported ably by Freda Elliott) walked away with the ladies' pairs, losing just one game in ten.

This normally unbiased commentator felt some stirrings of *hiraeth* and *hwyl* when both men's and women's fours were won by Wales – a uniquely magnificent performance.

GREAT ACHIEVEMENTS AT WORLD BOWLS AND COMMONWEALTH GAMES

David Bryant, the world's uncontested all-time number one, has won four Commonwealth Games singles gold medals – in 1962, 1970, 1974 and 1978; and two World singles golds – in 1966 and 1980. Ineligible for competition in 1982 and 1986, on the grounds of professionalism, a nifty redefinition of the word 'amateur' may let David (and others) back into the fold in 1990!

South Africa, a great bowls nation, swept the board in 1976, lifting singles, pairs, triples and fours titles – as well as the Leonard Trophy, of course. Cecil Bransky, now of Israel and regular TV performer, was the South African team reserve on that occasion.

Morgan Moffat, formerly a member of the Whitehouse and Grange Bowling Club in Edinburgh, won a bronze medal for Scotland in the Commonwealth Games at Christchurch in 1974. He stayed on in New Zealand – and now represents the

All Blacks at bowls, winning medals for his adopted country in 1978, 1980, 1982 and 1984!

Hong Kong, with only around 600 male bowlers, have won more gold medals at world level than their modest membership should entitle them to: pairs golds in 1972 and 1978 and fours golds in 1970, 1978 and 1980 are proof of amazing skill, temperament and teamwork.

Botswana and Guernsey, two more Cinderella competitors, won their first-ever medals at the Thirteenth Games at Edinburgh in 1986, taking the ladies' singles bronze and pairs silver respectively.

INDOOR – CLUB

THE WORLD INDOOR SINGLES CHAMPIONSHIP
BILL MALCOLM
BBC Sports Producer

The televising of indoor bowls started in Coatbridge, Scotland, in 1976, with the Monklands International BBC Indoor Tournament, a special invitation event which featured the respective champions of England, Scotland, Wales and Ireland.
The format remained the same until 1979, when the Embassy World Indoor Bowls Championship was inaugurated, after which the event has grown steadily in terms of the quality and number of players now invited to the Championship to play for the title and prize money. In 1987, 32 players – including nine from overseas – played for a first prize of £12,000 and the World title. The total prize money was £52,400.
Back in 1976 television coverage of the indoor bowls scene was very basic indeed: a total of three cameras – one at each end of the rink and one personality camera situated midway up the rink. There was no such sophistication as a commentary scaffold and commentary hut. The commentator was situated alongside the personality camera – not exactly ideal for describing the 'head' or which bowl lay 'shot', and a positive nightmare for trying to assess the strategy of the match being played.
Since those days, the BBC and the World Indoor Bowling Council (WIBC) have worked very hard at improving television coverage of the game for its millions of viewers. Much

time and thought has been given to various ways of improving the presentation of the sport on television. Advancement in modern technology has played its part and the new formula prevails.

Six cameras now cover the play and another two operate in the 'Linking Studio' – one high camera at each end of the rink, two personality cameras and two overhead HECTOR shots. HECTOR is a term devised by my engineering colleagues to describe a High Electronic Camera Travelling On Rails. Special rails and fittings were devised to allow the cameras to travel overhead, while still capable of being operated by cameramen situated on specially-built scaffold at each end of the rink. Commentators now have their own commentary hut at one end of the rink, over the head, and they also have the facility visually to illustrate to the viewers by means of a 'Telestrator' important information such as 'the problem bowl' or 'where the next shot should be placed'. These useful explanations help to make the game more interesting to the viewers at home.

Commentators' voices and remarks being overheard by the players still cause problems, but this has been improved immensely over the years. I can recall a situation during our coverage of the Scottish National Championships when the player was about to play his final bowl lying one shot down in the match. He had just made his decision as to how he was going to bowl his last shot, when he heard the voice of David Bryant comment, 'Well, he has only one shot he can play, he must play backhand' – a shot which was the complete opposite of what the player had in mind – and actually played!

The markers – referees – now have radio mics enabling the viewers to hear their opinions about who is lying the shot and other remarks to the players. The bowls have the same colour discs as the players' shirts, and the coloured lollipops all assist in giving information to the audience and viewers alike.

Years ago, critics and experts said bowling was an old man's game, and would not sustain hours of live television. But I always argued that, provided the standard of play was of a high quality and the commentary team were experts in the game – able to continue interesting conversation when the bowlers were walking 'to and from' the head – the viewers, especially the non-bowlers, could become fascinated with this very intriguing and skilful sport. My argument was accepted on a trial basis and I am pleased to see, over the years, that bowls is now acknowledged as a good, entertaining television sport alongside snooker and darts.

In 1987 Coatbridge Indoor Club hosted the ninth World Championship and indeed has been the venue for this event since its inception. Although the seating facilities are restricted, a special atmosphere exists with a very enthusiastic, knowledgeable bowling audience, which comes across very strongly on the screen and is very encouraging to the players.

Monklands Indoor Club, Coatbridge

Since the start of the World Championships, the clubhouse has been extended to allow for better facilities for the players, officials and sponsors. Prior to this extension, each section of the tournament had its own caravan parked in the car park. Players changed in one, council and bowling meetings were held in others and a little Scottish hospitality was known to have been dispensed from time to time. Many are the tales retold about the caravan days. The outstanding incident for me was the night when, because of the number of bodies indulging in hospitality all in the one caravan, it toppled at one end. Bodies, bottles and bowls were all thrown to the one end of the caravan and shouts of 'save the whisky' were heard. Thankfully, everyone and everything was raised to an upright position again, no injuries were reported and, mercifully, not a drop was spilled.

Although not yet a bowler, I am proud to have been associated with the pioneer work of establishing Indoor Bowls on television and would pay tribute to my late father, a past President of Croftfoot Bowling Club, for his insistence and encouragement that the great game of bowls should get more exposure on television.

WHAT HAPPENED NEXT?

In the inaugural year of the World Indoor Singles Championship in 1979, there was no prize money even though the tournament was televised. The format was a 'round robin' as was *Jack High*, but with only ten entries, and the first winner was of course David Bryant. The tournament was played in sub-zero temperatures and outside there was 9 inches of snow in some places. This caused quite a sensation for the overseas players. Erroll Bungay from Australia had never seen snow before and actually got himself up and out at 7.30 am to play in the snow.

The final was an entertaining affair as David Bryant's opponent was Jim Donnelly from Ireland who, in his early fifties, behaved like a 20-year-old, constantly running after his bowls and doing jigs round them. Jim sadly passed away between the 1979 and 1980 championships.

The championship stayed the same in 1980 and once again David Bryant was champion, beating Philip Chok in the final by 21–15. In 1981, the prize money was introduced by Embassy to a total of £6250, the winner receiving £2500 – a hat-trick for David Bryant against John Thomas 21–18. Television coverage was still restricted to a week after the event, but the championship then got the recognition it deserved. Almost by public demand, the tournament began its first daily TV coverage in 1982. Over twelve hours of bowling over seven days were transmitted, the 'round robin' was changed to knockout, the entries were increased from 10 to 16, and the prize money was increased almost two-fold to £12,000.

To the delight of the locals, the 1982 champion was John Watson who beat a young Irishman called Jim Baker in the final by 21–13. The Scots were cock-a-hoop again in 1983 when Bob Sutherland became champion in his home environment by beating Canadian Burnie Gill by 21–10 in the final. Burnie was, in fact, the shock name of the championship that year with some outstanding performances. In the first round he beat the up-and-coming Tony Allcock by 21–20 and to cap it all, went through to the second round by defeating the holder John Watson.

In 1984 Jim Baker took his revenge from two years before when he won the title, beating the young giant killer from Surrey, Nigel Smith, 21–18 in a truly magnificent game of bowls. The crowd gave them a standing ovation, particularly Jim Baker who began his bowling career at the age of 12, playing in short mat competitions in Ireland. The second indoor stadium in Ireland was also named after him. In 1985, the first visit to the World Indoor Singles was made by that colourful character Cecil Bransky of Israel. He made the final, only to be beaten 21–18 by Welshman and UK Champion Terry Sullivan.

All this time, from 1979 to 1986, the general public were waiting for a successor to the Master himself and in the 1986 World Singles, the star was born. Tony Allcock made his first appearance in the World Indoor Bowls in 1983, and was knocked out in the first round. Not so in 1986! He went through to become World Champion beating Noel Burrows (Crown Green) 21–18 in the quarter-finals and then disposing of both New Zealanders, Peter Belliss in the semi-final 21–17

Tony Allcock, World Indoor Singles Champion, 1986

and Phil Skoglund in the final 21–15. In the year 1986, the championship was upgraded to 24 entries and prize money was a massive £41,000, with the champion receiving £11,000. TV coverage had also increased from 12½ hours in 1982 to 17½ hours in 1986.

At the 1987 championships, other changes were made. The entries increased yet again to 32, the tournament went from 7–9 days, the format was altered from 21-up to sets, best of seven shots, and the prize money leapt once again to £52,400 with £12,000 to the winner. The final was a battle between the old and the new, Bryant and Allcock. The young pretender took the honours again winning by the closest margin of 5 sets to 4 sets in a best of 9 sets final.

This was to be the last year the World Indoor Singles took place at Coatbridge, as the game and the championship had begun to move on to even greater heights. Despite this major upheaval, most will agree that Coatbridge had an aura of its own and will never be forgotten. It can only be hoped that the new venue will be as successful in the coming years.

INDOOR – PORTABLE RINK

UK SINGLES AND WORLD PAIRS CHAMPIONSHIP
KEITH PHILLIPS

Indoor bowls clubs, which were usually housed in small, low-ceilinged halls, started around the turn of the 20th century and quickly became popular – particularly in Scotland, with its harsher winter weather. The indoor game quickly gathered momentum, so that when television became involved it was a highly organised part of the flat green scene.

In 1983, Mike Watterson – who had earlier been heavily involved with the televising of snooker – together with David Harrison, approached the Editor of Sport in Manchester, Nick Hunter, with another new offer for televised sport. The idea was to build a portable indoor bowls rink to take to large venues with auditorium areas, as in snooker, rather than the confined space of an indoor bowling club. It was hoped that this would attract the general public to come and watch in greater numbers and appeal to non-bowlers. It would also satisfy the needs of major sponsors, who would want quality facilities for entertaining customers. It was felt that this would take bowls into another era.

The World Indoor Singles Championship had started at Coatbridge in Scotland in 1979 and Mike Watterson wanted to develop the whole approach to indoor bowls for television. Nick Hunter was generally very enthusiastic about the idea of another major indoor bowls tournament and the British Isles Indoor Bowls Council gave the go-ahead for Mike and David Harrison to design and build a portable rink in time for the BBC to televise a brand-new competition, the UK Indoor Singles Championship, to be transmitted in November 1983.

Mike Williams, a Bristol designer, was given the job and in June a 120 × minimum 14-foot rink began to take shape. The 8 × 4-foot wooden pallets, arranged in threes across the rink, gave a width of 24 feet – and a playing surface of 18 feet.

The indoor portable rink – pallets lined up ready for assembly

Ninety pallets were interlocked with wedges, as in a snooker table, to make up the base. This was levelled with a laser device and jointed with a metal strip. The top surface was short strips of carpet, instead of one 120-foot piece, and David Bryant was asked to test it at a warehouse in Bristol. Overall his reaction was positive, so we seemed to have been given the green light to go ahead with the first UK Championship.

One major factor in the design of the portable rink was to be able to put it together in one day to cut down site costs. Consequently the location chosen was the Preston Guild Hall, known to the BBC to be the right size. The Guild Hall officials, under our old friends Vin Sumner and Alan Baker, were keen to co-operate. CIS agreed to sponsor and the competition was played in November 1983. Unfortunately, just before the tournament started, there was a technician's strike at the BBC and, despite management bravely manning cameras and sound equipment, it was decided to abandon the television transmissions which were due to cover the last four days.

The list of players for the first UK Championship included four crown green bowlers. This was partly done to satisfy the local community, as the venue is principally in crown green country. Only Noel Burrows and Allan Thompson, however, made it to the second round, with the final being won convincingly by David Bryant despite his opponent, Bob Sutherland, being the holder of the World, British Isles and Scottish indoor titles.

Another major innovation in this first television portable rink competition came from bowls itself. Jimmy Davidson, now established as a BBC-TV commentator, conceived a scoring method decided by sets. It would be ideal for television because each set would last between ten and forty minutes, already a successful timing in snooker transmissions. The best of three sets won the match, with the final best of five. The total prize money in 1983 was £16,800, with £4000 to the winner.

During the championship, problems arose with the portable rink. The carpet pallets were jointed with filler and the television lights caused them to lift. It was therefore decided to use an underlay for the first 1984 competition – the Granada Superbowl – so roofing felt was laid across the rink before the carpets were put on the surface. During the 1984 and 1985 competitions, different types of carpet and underlay were experimented with, but there were still problems with the carpet joins affecting the bias of the bowls.

The 1984 UK Championship was duly televised by the BBC – our first using a portable rink – and was won by Terry Sullivan of Wales. His passage through to the final was quite impressive, as he only dropped three sets, including a 3–1 win over the title holder David Bryant in the semi-final. However, to win the title he was against the up-and-coming star of the flat game, Tony Allcock. The match was a classic for BBC-TV's first televised indoor championship and went the whole distance. Eventually, Terry just managed to become the 1984 champion by winning five sets to four – a fitting climax to seven days of televised indoor bowls with excellent viewing figures. The TV indoor bowls game was obviously here to stay.

Terry Sullivan, winner of the 1984 UK Singles Championship

In 1985 the holder from Wales made an early exit, in the second round, to Scotland's John Watson – together with the 1983 champion David Bryant who lost to teenager John Rednall of England. Rednall made it to the semi-finals, only to lose to John Watson. Another youngster to make his name in this tournament was Scotland's Richard Corsie who also reached the semi-final stage, unfortunately losing to the eventual winner, jovial Jim Baker, in an exciting, close match. Jim had a relatively easy title win over John Watson in the best-of-nine-sets final. Once again the championship proved extremely popular with the viewing public, so much so that it was decided to launch another indoor championship.

Monday 7 April 1986 was the first day of the new Midland Bank World Indoor Pairs Championship. This brought significant changes to the indoor portable rink, building upon the experiences of the 1984 and 1985 seasons to try to iron out the problems once and for all. The top surfaces were completely changed and forty 12 × 6-foot panels were laid on to the base structure with carpet and a new thick underlay making only one joint, dead centre down the rink. This was ideal because the centre of the rink isn't used and therefore there would be no problems with alterations in the bias. The players commented on the rink, saying it was as good, if not better, than any other indoor bowling surface. The other distinct advantage was that the rink could be laid in an eight-hour period to a perfect surface 120 feet long. So from a three-day headache in 1983 to a one-day normality in 1987, a perfect rink has been built.

Returning to the World Indoor Pairs Championship of 1986, the new Bournemouth International Conference Centre was the chosen venue. The tournament was made a two-wood pairs rather than four woods per player, as it would be ideal for television timing, using the set format. It was also agreed that as players were going to be invited from around the world, a 'round robin' format would be used. This involved four teams in groups playing each other three times, with seven-up sets, and would prevent overseas players arriving and possibly only playing one game. Unfortunately the inevitable happened with this format and one group ended with a match which was 'dead', as the group had already been won. The players got together and decided to entertain the spectators with an exhibition match with a difference. It was to be a 'costume' match and Messrs. Bell, Ottaway, Allen and Baker, unbeknown to anyone – including the BBC production team – arrived on the

The four musketeers – l-r: Baker, Allen, Ottaway, and Bell

rink, John Bell looking particularly warlike and aggressive with a Viking costume and Jim Baker an excellent court jester. The crowd thoroughly enjoyed the match and it certainly dispelled the traditional image of flat green bowls being a boring old man's game. The title was eventually won by the two most popular men in the game, David Bryant and Tony Allcock.

Later that year the fourth UK Indoor Singles Championship took place at the Preston Guild Hall and, once again, the new-style portable rink behaved perfectly. The reigning champion, Jim Baker, was ousted in the first round by Welshman John Price, who went on to be beaten in the quarter-finals by Roy Cutts in a thriller over the whole five sets. A young, slightly portly Welshman by the name of Stephen Rees caused a sensation by defeating one of the favourites for the title, Tony Allcock, in the quarter-finals and then cheekily disposing of the 1986 Superbowl Champion, David Corkill from Ireland, in five sets to go through to the final against guess who? Yes that's right! Number one bowler, David Bryant.

David, who won the inaugural UK title in the non-televised championship of 1983, was considered to be favourite to take the title again. To everybody's astonishment, Stephen Rees raced to a 4–0 lead in the first session and the promoters were contemplating having to entertain the evening crowd with an exhibition match. But that wily old customer David Bryant is never beaten until the final bowl is bowled and had the evening crowd spellbound as he clawed his way back to 4–4. What a final! Stephen Rees managed to summon up some reserve strength for the deciding set and went on to win one of the most thrilling indoor finals seen on television.

Condolences to a great sportsman David Bryant, but what a wonderful happening for the game of bowls to have a young new champion. In fact, the average age of 1986's UK championship was younger than in the major snooker championships – which points to a great future for the game.

One interesting fact arising out of the UK Singles since 1983 is that only one crown green bowler has got past the second round stage: Brian Duncan, who reached the semi-final in 1984, to be beaten by Tony Allcock in four sets. Noel Burrows of course won the Superbowl in 1985. Even so, the crown green players have begun to influence the flat green bowlers' approach to the game. No longer is it just for fun and trips around the world. Money is now very high on the list of top flat green bowlers' priorities and they are developing the professional attitude to a now professional sport. Some crown green bowlers had played 500 matches by the time they played in Superbowl last year and this is rubbing off on to the new flat green stars.

The 1987 championship was dominated by the holders Bryant and Allcock and was played under a new format. Each round from the first to the semi-final was the best of 5 sets, 7 ends per set, as distinct from Singles being 7 up per set, and the final was the best of 9 sets, 7 ends per set.

David Bryant and Tony Allcock began as they meant to finish, particularly Tony Allcock, who couldn't put a foot wrong. Their first-round defeat of David Gourlay and John Watson was a clinical 3–0 victory, which was repeated throughout the rest of the tournament. They won their title once again, and in the process won 14 sets on the trot, never losing a set throughout, which will probably not be repeated.

England International bowler John Bell, who was part of the BBC-TV commentary team, said at the finish that it was the finest display of indoor bowling he had ever seen. The excellent crowd would certainly agree. Throughout the tournament the atmosphere was electric, and the total involvement of players and spectators alike was emphasised in *the* match of the championship: Alan McMullan and David Corkill of Ireland losing to the Welsh pair Stephen Rees and John Price 3 sets to 1. Unfortunately, the Welshmen couldn't match the devastating form of Allcock and Bryant in the final and were annihilated 5 sets to 0, the holders winning £13,000 between them.

CHAPTER 4

WHAT A LOT OF BOWLS

JOHN BELL
Professional Player

John Bell, England international, in action

27 April 1987 marks the first anniversary of the opening of my outdoor club – Wigton, in Cumbria. Every time I use its modern and spacious facilities I can't help but think that the dramatic development of our club is physical proof of the healthy nature of the game of bowls in general.

Up until 1986 this little club, which is situated in a small market town of some 5000 people, had only 50 members and an equally slender bank balance of £150. We, like many other clubs in the country, had persevered on a public park green with a small wooden clubhouse, which was literally a converted hen house donated by a generous member in 1970. Inspired by the desperate need to provide better facilities and to increase membership by tapping the obvious upsurge in interest in the game, the club acquired a piece of land, laid a new bowling green and commissioned the construction of a magnificent new clubhouse which must now rank among the finest in the north of England. The cost of the venture was reduced thanks to the stalwart physical efforts of a handful of members but it still reached the £100,000 mark. However, it was all worthwhile, because within four months of completion the membership had reached almost 200.

Our two neighbouring village clubs at Dalston and Aspatria with populations of only 5000 and 3000 respectively have also completed impressive new clubhouses during 1986, amounting to a further £120,000 of investment. The construction of a £200,000 extension to our local indoor stadium at Carlisle makes it the second largest indoor playing surface in the country and one which has attracted 350 new bowlers since its completion in December 1986.

This introductory glimpse at the interest and investment in the game of bowls in one small part of the English bowling associations' 'north-west frontier' illustrates perfectly the current buoyant nature of our beloved sport. This remote part of the country, whose early touring teams included the Romans and Vikings and more recently the EBA and EIBA, is traditionally low in population, rich in quality of life, but relatively poor in material wealth. Yet in 1986 a mere strip of 20 square miles has attracted investment of £420,000 and some 600 *new* bowlers into our noble game. Even more encouraging is the fact that this kind of activity is typical of developments throughout the British Isles.

What has happened to instil this new-found confidence and interest in the game of bowls? I am convinced the answer is related to the increased television exposure now given to the sport, as well as the vastly improved opportunities and incentives which exist for bowlers at every level of the game. Indeed the prestigious TV tournaments themselves represent some of the most attractive incentives to aspiring competitive bowlers, but even more significant to the development of the game is the role that TV exposure has played in eradicating that old mis-conception of bowls being an old man's game. The game's clean, sporting image and skilful nature have also been clearly highlighted through television coverage and this has succeeded in selling the game to the public in general, many of whom are becoming the bowlers of tomorrow.

The game to which they are being attracted is certainly very different to the one I entered as a chubby-faced but almost fit schoolboy in the early Sixties. Introduced to the game at the age of 13 by my father, a regular Cumberland County player, and encouraged by the members of the now defunct Wigton Throstle Nest Bowling Club, I was representing the club in league or friendly matches by the time I was 15.

The opportunities for personal development and the incentives to stimulate further endeavour and dedication have thankfully much improved since my early days. At the time of my entrance into bowls the number of teenage bowlers was very small and largely limited to those who, like myself, had been introduced to the game by a close relative. In fairness, the attitude towards us young hopefuls in those days was generally supportive. However, there was a distinct reluctance to allow boys to compete in a game that had previously been dominated by men. Many still needed to be convinced that boys could play the game properly or could avoid putting the Barnes Wallis bouncing bomb theory into practice. This restrictive attitude was reflected in the competition rules of that time where players in national competitions and major local tournaments had to be over 16 years of age. I can remember being prevented from playing in a local seaside tournament on the 'Costa Del Solway' because I was considered to be too young – even though I was playing regularly for my club. Elephantine bowlers never forget and I took extra pleasure in winning the tournament a few years later.

How things have changed today. Most counties have junior championships; national competitions for Under-25s (outdoor) and Under-31s (indoor) have been officially constituted and the age limit for national competitions has been reduced to 12. Club facilities have been generally improved to provide an abundant supply of attractive club premises with active social sections. Extensive TV exposure has accelerated the recruitment of new young bowlers and at long last it is generally accepted that bowls is a game where the keen faculties and attributes of youth are distinct advantages.

The new, acceptable image of the game now allows normal, fit teenagers openly to choose bowls as a sport in preference to football and rugby without their hormone composition being put into question. In the past many dutiful boys dabbled in the game of bowls to please their bowling fathers and mothers on payment of an increase in pocket money or a release from some horrific gardening task, but they seldom stayed the course. Football, cricket, rugby and other popular adolescent sports usually took precedence over the excitement of the bowling club aggregate night. This is happily no longer the case and the expanding opportunities and facilities are now not only attracting young bowlers for a trial period, but retaining their attention and participation.

This factor is crucial in securing a healthy future for the game both in terms of numbers supporting it and the quality of players emerging to represent and promote it. Competitive experience and a thorough grounding in the basic techniques are essential for the apprentice bowler. If this can be gained in your formative years it is invaluable. Naturally talented young players can then emerge on to the competitive scene with a thorough training behind them, and at an age when their bodies and minds are at their most alert and still relatively free of the rigours of the post-match celebration/consolation drinks and teas!

Whilst the encouragement and participation of young players is a key element in today's bowls scene it should not overshadow the fact that opportunities and incentives exist for all age groups. Players new and old, competitive or socially minded, can pursue their bowling desires and enjoy the game at whatever level they choose. County and national competitions have been gradually expanded with the aid of sponsorship to provide a complete range of choice for competition bowlers whether as individuals or club representatives.

Incentives mean different things to different people. There is no doubt that titles, both local and national, are powerful incentives, while the TV tournaments may now offer a glamorous and lucrative goal for both young and old bowling hopefuls. I still however believe that the greatest ultimate incentive in the sport for all purposeful bowlers is that coveted place in the national team. Selection for one's country is recognition of a consistently high level of performance and achievement over a period of time and in my opinion still constitutes the highest prize on the bowling circuit. I, like many of my international colleagues, have experienced no greater feeling of pride, satisfaction and emotion than when stepping on to the green to represent England. The electric atmosphere and sheer sense of international occasion during the British Isles championships are both exhilarating and totally penetrating. The experience and the opportunity of playing with and against class players in a sporting but extremely competitive situation is a great conditioner and character builder. Ability and temperament are tested to the full and the gladiatorial arena is no place for the weak.

Peter Brimble, the England Indoor team manager and one of the best motivators and analysts in the game, firmly preaches that 'the team with the most bottle wins'. This is borne out time and again at every playing level. In a closely fought contest the player who can withstand the pressure and nerves of the final stages of a game as well as that of the occasion itself will win the day. In these circumstances the weight of the situation can be considerably reduced by the compatibility and character of fellow team members.

Since I started my international career in 1978 I can recall many dramatic finishes and pressure situations. The World Championship Fours Final at Aberdeen in 1984 provided the tensest finish of my career and demonstrated perfectly the advantage of having a totally compatible and experienced playing unit.

With a World title at stake there is no way you can ignore the importance of the game. George Turley, Julian Haines, Tony Allcock and myself had battled our way to the fours final after winning nine of our ten sectional games. On a dark and wet Friday in July a hitherto mythical object – the World title – was within our grasp. We were playing New Zealand, a formidable four: Rowan Brassey, Jim Scott, Morgan Moffat and Phil Skoglund. The wet playing conditions were certainly more familiar to us than to our antipodean opponents and by the last end we had built a slender but significant lead of three shots. We needed bowls in the head and cover at the back. The dependable George and Julian provided both. Our title was looking more secure by the minute. Morgan Moffat fired with his first bowl and missed. I played another bowl into the head which looked to have locked into a safe position. Morgan unleashed a second driving bowl. He hit the head, the dust settled and in one incredible and awful moment we saw he had succeeded in removing all our bowls from the head.

We were now four shots down. The look on Julian Haines' face said it all. Fortunately he was too shocked to swear. George bit the end of his cigarette off and then swore. Tony and I looked at each other hoping for some divine word of consolation or inspiration. Suddenly cruel reality transformed a glorious occasion into the wet, miserable day it was. We agreed on my next shot. I was to try and push into the diagonal line of New Zealand shot bowls. I walked briskly down the green and driven on by sheer determination played the bowl quickly to avoid dwelling too much on the fact that it was the most important bowl I had ever played. The line of my bowl looked good, I broke into a trot – my fastest speed – and arrived just in time to see it turn out the first New Zealand shot bowl and stay in its place. My rink mates hugged me – if they had mugged me I wouldn't have noticed for we were shot again and almost champions. Phil Skoglund had to remove my shot bowl to save the game. He moved the jack with his last bowl but could only muster two shots. We were World Champions!

Those last few minutes of tension, exhilaration, disappointment, dejection and then sheer elation and mental relief will never be forgotten. There could not have been four happier bowlers anywhere in the world on that dark, damp day in July 1984.

The English team winning the 1984 World Fours final

Participation in the major international tournaments and championships, like World Bowls, where players spend long periods of time together, can give a great insight into the make-up and qualities, both in bowling and human terms, of fellow internationals. Over the last eight years I have had the pleasure and privilege of participating in a number of international tournaments both at home and abroad where I have been able to both play against, and socialise with, most of the world's leading bowlers. As the game rises in stature, and exposure to the general public increases, the image of the game will be increasingly influenced by the skills and character of these players who compete in the top-flight tournaments and championships. In my experience a lot of these players have enhanced the game of bowls by their own particular attitude, and of course their bowling ability. I will conclude by presenting a snapshot of some of the players I think have contributed something special to the game which is the richer for it.

Where on the bowls circuit has the combination of a 'warthog', 'stork', 'hippo' and a 'golden golly' won a major title? Aberdeen 1984. Those were the pseudonyms mutually bestowed on George Turley, Julian Haines, myself and Tony Allcock respectively. They were applied for our own amusement both on the rink and socially, and helped to cement the very happy and compatible relationship between us. A quick glance at the physical characteristics of each of us will soon explain the relevant creative associations: George's rugged northern looks, Julian's 72-inch inside leg measurement, my substantial carcass and Tony's fresh complexion and curly locks.

The contribution of Tony Allcock to our performance was tremendous. In Aberdeen he demonstrated all his best playing qualities – flair, natural ability, adventure and supreme confidence. He has continued to put these to good effect, enriching his reputation and the game in general. Tony plays a refreshing, adventurous game. He takes chances in going for shots but his confidence and outstanding ability ensures him a high success rate. He invariably provides an exciting game for spectators. He is a fast player; he wastes very little time and is keen to keep the game flowing. His accuracy and his reassurance and support for his colleagues are unending.

Our three weeks in Aberdeen existing as a team both on and off the green told us a lot about this talented young man. A naturally jovial person, Tony engages easily in amusing exchanges both during and outside games. This practice succeeds in reducing tension and pressure during matches and certainly at Aberdeen ensured our four played at ease with each other throughout the tournament.

The 1980 World Championships in Melbourne, Australia brought Tony his first world title – the Triples. Since then he has added another four – two World Indoor Singles, the World Indoor Pairs and the World Outdoor Fours. He is the hottest property currently on the bowls scene, and his special bowling skills are now entertaining and thrilling large television audiences. They will undoubtedly succeed in winning over even more viewers in the future. In any event there will be no one more appreciative or aware of those skills than his three World Fours colleagues – 'Warthog', 'Stork' and 'Hippo'.

Frequent association with many of the game's top names has allowed me a privileged look at their styles and outlook. As a result many characteristics of the game are instantly identifiable with certain players. Asked to provide the best examples of players who demonstrate 'determination' and 'genuine will to win' – two essential requisites for international competition – I would submit the names of Willie Wood and David Gourlay of Scotland.

I have played against both men and watched them on many occasions. England has dominated the home internationals over the last four years but, prior to this, Scotland ruled the roost for several years. The skipping performances of David and Willie made a significant contribution to this success. Their national pride, enthusiasm for the game and a dogged determination to win make them extremely difficult opponents and much revered in bowls. They play the game in a very competitive yet sporting manner – and generate a great sense of presence. They were Commonwealth gold medallists in 1982, bringing back their titles from Australia in the face of strong opposition from the host nation and the New Zealand team, who were playing under conditions much more suited to them than to the Scots. This says a lot for the calibre of the Scots pair.

Willie Wood is no stranger to overseas success. A Mazda win in 1983 and brilliant performances in the Hong Kong International Classic Pairs, with George Adrain, secured that title two years in succession – 1985 and 1986. This achievement also ensured him some special treatment at the final presentation dinner in 1985. Willie had made no secret of the fact that his Gifford palate and stomach were not coping too well with oriental delicacies such as abalone (sea-slug), seaweed soup, squid and the like. As a result the Hong Kong Lawn Bowling Association had a large plate of 'mince and tatties' prepared and served exclusively for Willie.

Mention 'standby' air tickets and cockroaches to David Gourlay and you are assured of an instant response of Gaelic swear-words. David and I were sent tickets for our travel to New Zealand for their Countrywide Classic. These turned out to be 'standby' tickets, ie you only get on the plane if there are spare seats. We were informed at Los Angeles that if we got to Honolulu standby passengers there had been waiting to get out

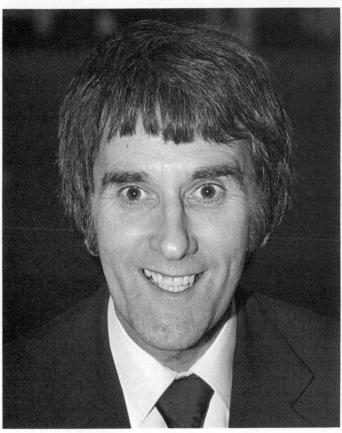

David Gourlay, Scottish international skipper

for over a fortnight. We were, in fact, two of the last four passengers to be called at Honolulu. You might not see David looking worried too often on the bowling green but he was worried that day. However, in retrospect, the prospect of a few weeks in Honolulu surely cannot have been *too* off-putting!

During the Fiji classic in 1986 David happened to have a hotel room which was obviously close to a nest of enormous South Pacific cockroaches which paraded continually across his room all through the night. His wife Sarah was terrified of them and David had to stay up all night standing guard. Armed with a shoe he depleted their numbers somewhat, but failed to wipe them out. Hence the expression in the cockroach world – caught by the Gourlays!

One of my most enjoyable overseas trips was my first visit to the Newcastle International Classic Pairs in Australia, which was also my first overseas trip. My partner was the one and only Mal Hughes who, along with his Hartlepool colleague George Turley, epitomises another important aspect of the game – the caring, supportive element in bowls. Both men encourage and generate good team spirit both on and off the green and are renowned throughout the bowling circuit for their warmth and approachable nature. Above all, they not only teach you how to play the game but how to enjoy it. Mal Hughes oozes personality. His charisma soon influences his playing colleagues and quickly establishes a relaxed climate in which to play the game. I had the pleasure of playing with Mal in the Newcastle Pairs, the 1980 World Championships and in the outdoor England team. The way he, as a skipper, encourages his players and avoids any reference to poor play is an example to all.

Playing in Australia is a marvellous experience and must represent one of the best incentives in the game. The Newcastle Pairs is a feast of bowling and Australian hospitality. The temperature averaged 80–90 degrees, just like Cumbria on August Bank Holiday! The greens are unbelievably smooth and true. They are more akin to our indoor surfaces than our greens in terms of appearance and performance. The Australian clubhouses are enormous and luxurious. The greens are very fast, requiring a week at least of acclimatisation. All British participants are instantly recognisable by their bright pink hue! It was difficult to convince us that the sun was 93 million miles away. Large insects of enormous proportions buzzed around, and large wild parrots squawked incessantly from the trees, providing a good impersonation of a ladies' friendly match!

Against this backcloth Mal and I went unbeaten through the tournament, and after an exciting final against the pair from South Australia – Wally Bonaguro and Verd Hamblen – we emerged 18–11 winners. This has been the only time the title has been taken out of Australia, and a year later we took fourth place in the World Pairs in Frankston. We were a very happy and compatible pair. Our similar sense of humour and our belief in the enjoyment of life in general contributed no small part to our teamwork. Once again the value of compatibility to a successful performance was proved beyond doubt.

Mal Hughes explaining a technical point to David Icke

An examination of the game of bowls would not be complete without reference to the man who in my opinion has done more for the game than anyone else in the world – the Master himself, David Bryant. He has won everything there is to win – more than once in most cases. His name is synonymous with the game of bowls. His appetite for the game is as keen as ever and his playing ability equally so. Yet it is David Bryant's conduct and attitude that deserve most attention and appreciation. With all his success he has set a splendid example as a figurehead for our sport. He has won and lost with dignity and grace. He has never outgrown the sport or isolated himself from his colleagues, and for that the game and its players are the richer. David, together with Willie Wood, officially opened my club's new green last April. The town and a lot of Cumbria's bowlers turned out in force to see it. David was treated as a long-lost brother by the assembled throng, many of whom were not bowlers. He was besieged for most of the weekend. He must have signed hundreds of autographs but he undertook his task willingly and with enthusiasm. That is David Bryant.

Not long ago I presented the prizes for a local domino league in West Cumbria. One large ex-rugby player approached me and said how impressed he was with the bowling on TV and how well the sport is doing now. He concluded that it is now so popular that 'Bill Bryant is a household name'. I told 'Bill' the next time I saw him. He was greatly amused and we often have a good laugh over it. For David Bryant's contribution to the game of bowls I sincerely thank him.

Our beloved game of bowls has changed considerably. Television, increased participation and the resultant demands are boosting it by the month. Further refinements will inevitably take place in the continual attempt to make it more attractive and appealing to viewer and player alike. Radical alteration to the game is, however, unnecessary. The game is thriving, packed with opportunity, and has a healthy future. New bowlers, young and old, are being successfully recruited, the basic integrity of the sport has a very solid foundation and current investment in the game is considerable. This happily means that players at every level of the game can benefit and above all be proud to be part of one of the finest sports available to every age-group.

CHAPTER 5

STARS OF THE FLAT GAME

KEITH PHILLIPS

JIM BAKER

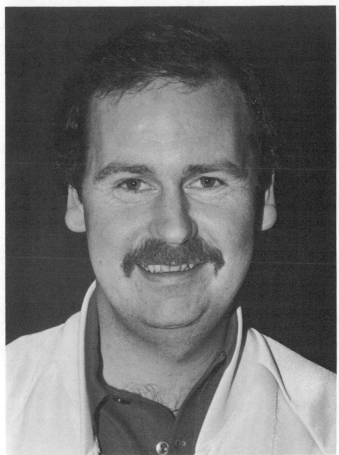

Jim Baker, 1985 UK Indoor Singles Champion

Jim, 29, has been an international since 1979 in both indoor and outdoor bowls and comes from an Irish bowling family. Manager of an indoor bowling stadium, he has a wonderful jovial personality and is one of the most popular bowlers in the game. He has a natural ability in the bowling green which has brought him international success and honours, and consequently the stadium at Templepatrick close to Belfast was named after him.

His two most important titles were won in BBC televised competitions. His win at Coatbridge in the World Indoor Singles Championship in 1984 showed how he beat the 'jinx' there for players over-relying on the drive to get them through or out of trouble. It was this single factor in the final stages of the World Indoor Singles in 1984 that contributed the most to his title win, as he out-drove everyone else. In that year he also became World Triples Champion.

Jim doesn't always rely on his skill at driving to achieve his championship wins, as was proved at the UK Indoor Singles in 1985. In the final on the portable rink at Preston, Jim was two sets to nil down in the best of nine sets when he realised that his opponent John Watson wasn't managing to hit the line on short jacks. Jim changed his tactics and won the match by five sets to two. I'm sure Jim Baker will continue to be in the top rankings for many years to come.

TONY ALLCOCK

Tony, 32, and a head teacher at a school for handicapped children, won his first county title in the Leicestershire Pairs at the age of 17 in 1972. Since then, he has never looked back, winning many international honours as well as major titles. He has won gold medals for triples in the World Championships in 1980, was skipper for the World Fours to win the gold and won a silver in the Pairs in 1984 at Aberdeen.

Currently the most successful bowler in the world, he was reportedly 'carried' by his late mother Jean, an international bowler, on the green before he was born. Since that inauguration to bowls, he has become the champion of the people who fill the venues to see his inimitable style of play. Because of this, coaches of the game are in despair: he is unorthodox compared to his pairs partner David Bryant, who bowls the 'right' way. David's rigid preparation is followed by definite follow-through, whereas Tony plays like the majority of crown green bowlers: no preparation, just down and deliver immediately with no follow-through whatsoever. Tony has won his first coaching certificate and, much to the dismay of coaches who insist that a good follow-through is a 'must' for any bowler to succeed, recounts that in his teaching of the mechanics of a good bowls delivery action it is a case of 'do as I say' and not 'do as I do'!

Tony has reached the stage where Steve Davis was a few years ago in snooker, where he could do no wrong and was unbeatable. His winning performance with David Bryant in the World Indoor Pairs at Bournemouth in 1987 was remarkable and even David would admit he was carried to a large extent in this tournament.

In the last two years, Tony Allcock has won the World Indoor Singles title twice and paired with David Bryant to win the World Indoor Pairs two years in succession. On his form, he should win the TV Indoor Grand Slam adding the UK Indoor Singles title in October 1987.

DAVID BRYANT

What can you say about the Master that hasn't already been said? David Bryant, 56, is one of the greatest sporting ambassadors this country has known as well as the greatest bowler of all time, and he's still there on finals day at most of the major competitions. It was 40 years ago that he won his first title at the age of 16 and since then he has been the most prolific winning bowler in the world. Quite simply, his record is outstanding.

David was Commonwealth Singles Champion for an unbroken period of 20 years, then was unable to defend his title in 1982 because he declared himself a professional. The most staggering statistics were from 1970–1973. The entries for the English Outdoor Singles exceed 10,000 each year. Bryant started in Round 1 each year and won the title three years running and again in 1975. Not only that, he did the same in the British Isles Singles; three years running 1971–3 against the total entries from Wales, Scotland and Ireland as well as England. A truly remarkable feat!

These, of course, were outdoor tournaments in relatively earlier days. In 1979, David started to dominate the televised

Allcock and Bryant, 1985 and 1986 World Indoor Pairs Champions

indoor tournaments by winning the World Singles three years running in 1979–81, then, in 1983, the UK Singles. More recently, he was runner-up in the UK Singles final in 1986, losing out to Welshman Stephen Rees by four sets to five after trailing 0–4. In February 1987 he was runner-up in the World Singles, beaten by Tony Allcock after holding a match winning lie at 4–3, only to lose four sets to five again. But in March 1987 he had some consolation by winning the World Indoor Pairs with Tony Allcock five sets to nil.

PETER BELLISS

Peter, 36, started bowling at the age of eight with his mother and father, and in 1970 at the age of 19 won his first Singles title in New Zealand. Since then, he has won at least one title every year on his home ground, as well as international honours since 1982, when he won a bronze medal in the Commonwealth Games at Brisbane. Peter is the current World Singles Champion (Outdoors), and in 1986 was losing semi-finalist in the World Indoor Singles against Tony Allcock.

Peter is acknowledged as one of the best drivers in the game and it was one such drive that gained him the World Singles title at Aberdeen in July 1984. He is also one of the best

Peter Belliss, winner of the World Singles title, 1984

exponents of the clean, smooth delivery which he has developed on the fast greens of New Zealand.

Earlier that year in June, Peter was beaten by David Bryant in the final of the *Jack High* tournament at Beach House Park, Worthing. He stayed on in this country to learn to master the British greens which are much slower paced than in New Zealand, before playing in the World Championships at Aberdeen. This was to be a memorable final as the score at the final end was 20–20 against Scotland's hero, Willie Wood.

Willie was lying shot bowl and Peter had the last bowl of the match. He drove and removed Willie's shot bowl which meant a measure for the title. Tension mounted as the new sonic measure was used but it was not decisive so it was discarded. A conventional spring measure gave Peter Belliss the title.

THE CROWN GAME

CHAPTER 6

A HISTORY OF CROWN GREEN BOWLING

HARRY RIGBY
BBC Bowls Commentator

The essential difference between flat and crown green bowling is the surface on which the game is played. Crown greens are undulating, with bumps known as crowns. Some greens have just one, others may have two or three and they can be up to 14 inches high from edge to centre. On the other hand flat greens, known as rinks, are on a large surface of grass as level as it possibly can be. On one area there can be many rinks of around 16 feet wide and 120 feet long. This is the standard flat green rink size and can only vary very slightly.

Since television took an interest in bowls, both flat and crown codes are providing participants for the new indoor flat green competitions and it is significant that the crown green bowlers are taking to the flat, whilst the flat green bowlers rarely venture into the crown green world. This is obviously because it is easier to adapt to flat green rinks due to their one standard size and width. It is extremely difficult to build indoor crown greens as it's almost impossible to stop the bowls from rolling down into the ditch. Until a surface is designed that has the braking power of standard outside turf greens, the crown game is committed to outdoors only.

It is because of the vast differences of surfaces that the methods and techniques of both codes, including equipment, are far apart. Crown green bowlers have to concentrate so much on beating the green that they don't rely too heavily on tactics and strategy, but aim to get as close to the jack as possible. Flat green bowlers, on the other hand, have a much easier task to reach close to the jack, as their rink is a constant size and width. Consequently they dwell heavily on the tactical side of preventing their opponent scoring.

How crown green developed as a separate game is difficult to pinpoint, but my preferred theory is that bowling from the 15th century to the 18th century separated into two classes. The rich and the moneyed who owned large gardens made bowling alleys on their lawns, flanked by hedges – in other words, rinks. The less affluent played on common ground and parks close to inns and taverns, which were the forerunners of the crown greens built adjacent to pubs and hotels.

It is hard to say when crown green became properly organised, but Lancashire was certainly a leading force in the 19th century. Blackpool Sweepstakes started in 1878 and it is worth noting that in 1897 Lancashire and Cheshire combined for the first time and played Warwickshire and Worcester in a series of county games. These ended in 1903 and four years later the British Crown Green Amateur Association was formed. There were already quite a number of other associations in existence, including Cheshire, Manchester and District, Liverpool, Huddersfield, Leeds, Spen Valley, plus public parks and licensed victuallers' leagues and many others.

The crown green game has continued to grow since 1907. Its boundaries now stretch from Cumbria in the north to Worcestershire in the Midlands. It grew first from eight counties to ten, and in 1987, 14 English counties make up the body of the British Crown Green. They are Cheshire, Cumbria, Derbyshire, Greater Manchester, Lancashire, Merseyside, North Lancashire and Fylde, North Midlands, Potteries, Shropshire, Staffordshire, South Yorkshire, Warwick and Worcestershire, Yorkshire, together with Wales. The BCGAA now has a National Coach, ex-Coventry City footballer Harry Barrett, plus two delegates to the English Bowls Council. A delegate from each county attends a full council, while the management and committee are formed from the county delegates, with a secretary, treasurer and an assistant secretary.

Crown green bowling is an excellent game and, if anybody is thinking it's too minor a sport, there are thousands of crown greens in Britain and they are all in full use! There's no doubt that television has had a great influence, and increased the public interest in the game. It is also as well to note that bowls, flat and crown, is a relatively easy game to learn – but, like all other sports, hard to be good at. Many younger people are playing the game and holding their own in the senior ranks. Handicaps are on the increase and springing up all the time.

Unfortunately this has brought some problems with too many competitions being organised. Some of the top officials think it has reached saturation point. The top bowlers, particularly the professionals who rely on the game for a living, are sometimes travelling through three counties in a day to play in three simultaneous tournaments. They have even found themselves in two different finals on the same day, on different sides of the country! Having to opt to play in one final, they obviously go for the richest prize money – which leaves the other final a walk-over. This doesn't do much for the organiser's headache, as he's probably advertised the two finalists. The game is trying to overcome this problem and there is now a diary available to all crown green bowlers showing all competitions with dates of every round.

'Seven days a week is not enough' is so often the cry of the over-committed crown green bowler. Not so long ago he would have had to manage with six days and to have suffered some harassment if he had tried to make it seven. While it seems normal now that bowls should be played on a Sunday, it wasn't always so. The Lord's Day Observance Society wanted to keep Sunday free from sport of any kind, and as the two sides prepared to do battle, the bowlers found that the Church, the Law and the Establishment were lined up on the side of the Observance Society.

However, in 1962, Threlfalls Breweries, now Whitbreads, opened their bowling greens in Manchester, Salford and Liverpool for the first time on a Sunday. Floodlit bowling was in the offing, outdoor winter bowling was just beginning to develop in popularity, handicap bowling was starting to flourish and television was to bring the game to a wider public and foster further changes that could never have happened without it. Most of the top crown players were, at the time, actually prejudiced against anything but singles, but television, and money, changed all that.

The way crown green bowlers played, the way that they dressed, and the way that they thought about the game was to change too. Only now are they coming to accept that the other half of the game – the flat green – is not quite as easy as they imagined it to be, and that flat players are not the easy pushover that, in their great wisdom, the crown green players prophesied they would be if ever the twain should meet. Now the realisation is gradually dawning upon the crown men that not only have they been playing only one facet of the game but that, in their own insular way, they have restricted themselves to just one section – namely singles.

The attitude to bowling on Sunday was just one of the many changes which took place in crown green bowling from the late 1950s and early 1960s. The Professional Panel Bowler's Association was a tightly-knit organisation and a law unto itself, and it held a firm, uncompromising grip on the bright stars of bowling who came under its authority. But the changes in the game at this time loosened even its hold and players like Brian Duncan, Norman Fletcher and Vernon Lee were able to move out into what was eventually to become the more lucrative area – the flat game.

The advent of television was undoubtedly the prime influence. It replaced the Panel as the platform of the stars. The players who appeared on the screen became the 'known' players. It was television that really put an end to the harassing of Sunday bowlers, bringing Sunday sport to a wider public and changing the public's attitude to sport on Sunday generally.

One very important figure in the development of crown green bowls is undoubtedly Eddie Elson, secretary to the

Eddie Elson, ex-secretary to the BCGBA

BCGBA. He sees his greatest achievement in his time in the 'hot seat' to have been his success in persuading the BCGBAA to go open, hence dropping the word 'amateur' from its title. This enabled the game to go for sponsorship with prize money and, more importantly, build up its television coverage.

The first controversial move was to change the name of the All England British Crown Green Merit Championship to suit the sponsors. This caused an uproar, but Eddie stood fast and won the battle. Hence the first sponsored event was known as the Watney Webster Merit and continued under that title for a number of years. One of the most successful sponsorships negotiated by Eddie was the Tom Thumb Champion of Champions tournament played at the Waterloo Hotel in Blackpool.

The huge popularity of the first championship in 1974 took the Waterloo by surprise. It wasn't long before the sponsors realised that this downmarket sponsorship was really up-market, with *Grandstand* television coverage, and they changed the name firstly to the John Player and later to the Embassy. Many stars of the crown green world have their name on the trophy. Tony Poole twice – in 1976 and 1984 – Noel Burrows twice – in 1978 and 1980 – but, surprisingly, no Brian Duncan or Dennis Mercer. Unfortunately, Embassy dropped out in 1985 and since then the competition has ceased to be televised.

THE LAWS OF THE GAME

A major contribution of Eddie Elson to the crown game was his part in consolidating a single set of rules wherever you played, with the help of Jack Uttley and Jack Isherwood.

Basically, the laws of the game have changed little in the last 50 years, alternatives and additions being made to meet situations arising through the spread of the game. A major overhaul took place in 1979 to update the laws and ensure all bowling was played under these rules as laid down by the governing body – the British Crown Green Bowling Association. Up until then there were many local variations, notably the so-called 'Blackpool Rules', which allowed two casts of the jacks and stamping, ie efforts to accelerate the progress of a bowl. Another local rule in many competitions was the use of a player's own jack, which could vary considerably in bias. Realising that it was in the best interests of the game as a whole, Eddie's recommended changes were accepted – including standardisation of jacks to two full bias. Since 1980 there have been no changes in the laws of the game, possibly the longest period for many years.

There are 41 laws, which are wide-ranging and cover all aspects of the game. As in all sports there are times when an odd incident occurs not specifically covered by a particular law – such as if a strong wind blows a jack off the green. However, to cover every possibility would require a whole volume. The following basic laws are framed to cover singles and pairs; seldom are other combinations played.

1 The leader shall bowl the jack to set a mark which if it rests on the green must be a distance of not less than 24 yards.

2 The opponent may make objection after the first bowl has been played, a measurement then takes place to decide the objection.

3 The method of scoring is one point for each bowl nearer to the jack than an opponent's.

4 No player is allowed to change the jack or bowls unless they are so damaged as to be unplayable.

5 If a jack or a bowl in its course is impeded in any way, they are returned to be replayed, but if a player impedes a running bowl both his bowls are forfeited at that end.

6 At the conclusion of an end, neither the jack or any bowl which is claimed to count is allowed to be moved without the consent of the opponent.

7 If a player about to deliver a bowl inadvertently drops it and cannot recover it without quitting the footer, the bowl is considered dead and taken out of play.

One of the most controversial aspects of the game prior to 1980 was the condonement of the practice of 'stamping' the foot alongside a bowl to endeavour to gain a few more yards. This was never allowed under BCG Rules, but was widespread in many competitions – particularly in the north-west. It is now completely outlawed and after one warning and the loss of a bowl, the offender may have his bowls taken off the green and the game awarded to his opponent.

Not all players are in agreement with the law which penalises a player – by loss of a bowl – for bowling a bowl other than his own; many think it should be replaced with the proper bowl. As yet no significant effort has been made to change the law.

Referees are instructed to insist and see that games are played in accordance with the laws of the game, and, should any dispute arise during a game which is not covered by the laws, the referee must make a decision which is final. By and large, if the spirit and intention of the laws of the game are adhered to, there should be little or no trouble. It is only when players seek to interpret the laws to gain unfair advantage that problems arise.

Jimmy Davidson outlined the basics of the game of bowls in a previous chapter. I will now attempt to highlight some of the principal differences between the two forms of bowling, as seen through the eye of a crown green man.

There are several fundamental differences. Crown green bowling is strictly an outside game. Greens on average are between 40–45 square yards in size; they consist of an uneven surface of well-manicured grass. By contrast, flat rinks have an even surface and the bowls are played up and down a lane without much variation.

Here are some of the most important variations between the two codes from the crown green players' angle, plus one or two thoughts that puzzle crown enthusiasts. Crown bowls are anything from 2lb 4oz to 3lb in weight; the lighter and smaller bowls are in the main used by ladies or juniors. Bowls are of wood or composition material and are made slightly off-centre or eccentric as this keeps a heavier weight mass on one side and this is known as bias. The most popular weights are 2lb 8oz–2lb 12oz.

By contrast, flat green bowls are much larger, starting at around 3lb and moving up to 4lb. Also the bias is much more pronounced and they are stronger than crown green woods. Crown green players use just two woods whereas the flat players use four. This obviously leads to the many variations in play. For example, the strategic placing of bowls round the end or head is much more pronounced in flat green because they have more chances of altering or retrieving a situation. People watching on TV often ask why some of the crown green ends seem much farther away from the jack than the flat green. The reason is that the variations on the flat rink are nowhere near as pronounced as they are on the crown greens.

Obviously crown greens all vary, due to the undulations and gullies. Therefore it is possible to place the jack in certain parts of the green and not bowl a wood less than a yard away from the jack. In both codes the jack is very important because the scoring of the games revolves around which bowls are nearest to it. In crown green, should both bowls from the same player be nearest, they both count one point each. If only one is nearest it is one point only, the same applying in flat green using four bowls (just double up). But there is a wide difference in the use of the jack. Flat green players use a composition ball similar to a cue ball in snooker. A mark is set by merely rolling it down the rink and if necessary at the players' requests, the jack can be handled by the official and moved from its original resting place.

Crown green people find this mystifying, for the jack in crown green bowling is an extremely valuable piece of equipment, governing the whole pattern of the game. It is a smaller replica of the bowls, about 23oz in weight, and is, like the bowls, eccentric in shape, and biased. It is used to determine the length (which could be anything from 19 yards to 75 yards in any direction), the speed of the green, the bias or peg and the weight or pace. Once it has been led out it must not be disturbed at all unless it is interfering with another end or some other infringement covered by British Crown Green rules. There are some really good jack handlers in the crown green game and their correct manipulation of the 'chitty', 'monkey', 'block', 'little un' (some of the nicknames it goes under) has been the difference between winning and losing! It goes without saying that the flat game players are superb at their game; their ability is beyond question, but the standards are just as high in crown green bowling. However, there is no doubt that the flat game looks better on TV because the bowls are more often played closer to the jack.

I would love to see a contest between all the top men of bowls (both codes) on a full-size flat rink under crown green rules. It would be thrilling to watch and I wouldn't like to tip the winner!

CHAPTER 7

THE CROWN GAME ON TELEVISION

KEITH PHILLIPS

THE WATERLOO

The year was 1907. The place was the Waterloo Hotel, Blackpool, and on a 45-yard square of the highest quality lawn turf, the most prestigious event in crown green bowling was born. There were 320 entries, the total prize money was £25 and the winner was Jas Rothwell from West Leigh, who beat the local hero from South Shore, Blackpool, T. Richardson. This was to be James Rothwell's only appearance in a Waterloo final, whilst the runner-up in the first Waterloo Handicap was to be losing finalist twice more, in 1919 and 1944.

In 1986 there were 2048 entries, the winner receiving £2000 out of £13,600 total prize money and this was Brian Duncan, the crown green king of the Seventies and Eighties and one of only three bowlers to have won the trophy twice, the first time

Waterloo Hotel bowling green, 1902

Arthur Murray, one of only three bowlers to win the Waterloo twice

being in 1979. The other two are Arthur Murray in 1973 and 1978, and Bernard Kelly in 1953 and 1954, the only bowler to have won the Waterloo two years in succession.

Over the 78 years this competition has been held, it has developed into the top event in the crown green bowling calendar and is now commonly known as the Cup Final of bowling played at the Wembley of crown green, the Waterloo Hotel, Blackpool. It is almost impossible to obtain tickets for the two final days and the event is a sell-out almost as soon as the previous year's final is over.

The bowling club itself has changed dramatically since that day in 1907 and throughout the years stands have developed round the green to make it the only crown green bowling stadium in Britain. In fact, over the last three years, the brewery owners of the stadium, Greenall Whitley, have spent over a quarter of a million pounds building two new stands, a brand-new cantilever stand on the west side that can hold 1200 and

Jas Rothwell, first Waterloo winner in 1907

a slightly smaller conventional stand on the east side, 677 capacity, to replace the glass verandah blown down in gales in February 1983, as well as refurbishing and improving the facilities—and there's more to come this year.

However, by far the more dramatic changes have been on the green itself since Jas Rothwell took that first title. Dress and equipment have changed considerably. In the early days dress was considered unimportant, with the bowlers arriving straight from their jobs with their bowls in their overcoat pockets, or the luckier ones in their 'dorothy' bags. Nowadays, with television and sponsorship, there is a smart uniform of sweater, flannels and shoes with the bowls in smart leather cases. A word about 'dorothy' bags. It is rumoured that a bowler's wife named Dorothy was fed up with her husband's bulging overcoat pockets. She decided 'if you can't beat 'em, join 'em' and made a special bag out of coat sleeves to keep his bowls in!

T. Richardson with 'dorothy' bag at the Waterloo Hotel

Another aspect of the crown green game at the Waterloo which has changed dramatically is the form of measuring a disputed end. Until 1981, when Jack Leigh took over as the bowling manager of the Waterloo Hotel, players were allowed to opt for 'cutting the straw' measuring. A player was allowed five minutes maximum to measure, the jack leader having the decision to the form of measuring. A straw was taken from a bunch and cut to the distance from the bowl to jack. Obviously, as the bowls are spherical, the straw had to be cut at an angle to get tight on to the bowls, the more experienced players developing an art in the angle and the length.

Jack Leigh, Waterloo Bowling Manager from 1981

Unfortunately this was prone to gamesmanship as some players bent the straw 'accidentally' in removing it from the measure. This happened to Noel Burrows in 1974 when playing veteran Billy Dawber. Billy opted for a straw measure and the straw was 'bent' when handed to Noel, who swears he lost an eighth of an inch in trying to straighten it out. The method is no longer used in major competitions and in the last year a new electronic device has been invented and is being used now in both flat and crown codes.

Straw measuring – still used today in some panel tournaments

Notable winners of the Waterloo include a former greyhound trainer, Bill Lacy of Wigan – one of the original cloth cap brigade, who in 1957 had a storming win over Tommy Bimson of St Anne's 21–7. The score doesn't do justice to the quality of that final, which was reckoned to be one of the best ever. Over 3500 enthusiasts who watched that match will never forget Bill Lacy playing with his trouser bottoms tucked into his stockings, which he said was 'the most memorable moment in my life'. He nearly claimed the elusive Blackpool double three days later, narrowly losing in the Talbot Final. And that was at the ripe 'young' age of 76!

Another stalwart of the green was George Barnes of Westhoughton, who used to start favourite whenever he went out. He thought nothing of playing for £25–£50 a side, with thousands being waged on his name elsewhere. Yet, despite reaching the finals twice, he never won the Waterloo.

There were the three Yorkshire winners: John Peace (1911), Tedber Tinker (1944) and Albert Ringrose (1948) who won £60 first prize and a further £600 in bets on himself from the first round to the final. All three were members of the Huddersfield brigade who regularly try for the Waterloo each autumn. One Huddersfield bowler is quoted as saying, 'I used to dream of taking Jane Russell to the Savoy and doing things that are unprintable, but now I'm older and wiser, my ambition is for a fairy godmother to grant me a couple of wishes. One to win the Waterloo and two to celebrate with halibut and chips at the Lobster Pot.'

It takes something pretty drastic to prevent the Waterloo taking place. Since 1907 the competition has only missed two years, 1910 and 1939, when the tournament was abandoned due to war being declared two weeks before finals day. Only once since then has the finals day been in jeopardy. In 1976 the heavens opened on the day of the semi-finals and final. By the time Keith Illingworth and Stuart Buckley stepped on the sacred turf to start battle for the first prize the green was covered in large pools of water. It was about the fifth final BBC-TV had covered and was live on Wednesday afternoon. We were extremely concerned as to whether the match would proceed, but the decision was made without hesitation. Game on. It became a throwing final rather than a bowling final and commentator Harry Rigby's description 'they're cobbing their bowls' became a national bowling phrase overnight. The 1976 final is now affectionately known as the Watersplash Final.

Since BBC-TV started covering crown green bowling's major event, there have been some great characters on show, performing in unforgettable finals. The unique Watersplash Final of 1976 was followed, in 1980, by the tussle between the 'Dancing Major' Vernon Lee from Blackpool, a local hero, and Glynn Vernon from Winsford in Cheshire. Lee, famous for his antics during bowling, gave a star performance, delighted the packed stadium, and won his first and only final 21–20 to become a most popular champion.

In post-war years, perhaps the most popular winner came from arguably the best final, the Streaker Final of 1982. The late Dennis Mercer from Stockport, a champion bowler in his own right, had a very difficult match against Ken Strutt from

Oldham. It was close all the way, and at 19–20 in favour of
Mercer, millions of TV viewers were to see a grandstand finish.
Ken put two close to the block and looked a certain winner.
But, forever optimistic, Dennis held on to the mat as they
approached the gathering of bowls. Suddenly, the second of
Ken Strutt's bowls fell over away from the jack and Dennis
immediately called for a measure. Ken was left with only one:
20–20. By now both spectators and viewers were on the edge of
their seats. Dennis Mercer deftly took the next end and fulfilled
his life's ambition, Waterloo champion 1982 in his first and
only final. You couldn't have scripted a better finish for such an
emotional occasion.

The Waterloo has come a long way since 1907, as steadily
increasing entries have meant an increase in the total prize
money. In 1987 this total will be increased to more than
£20,000, a crown green record, with £2500 to the victor and
£75 for being in the last 64 – all this for an entry fee of £4.50.
To join the Waterloo club costs only £2 a year and
consequently 25,000 bowlers use the green every year and 20
major events are played annually. Entries are now even
beginning to roll in from flat green country as far afield as
Scotland, London, Newcastle and across the water in Belgium.

It's quite a job for Jack Leigh to sort out the entries, which he
gets 18 months before the next competition: April 1986 for the
1987 Waterloo in September. Each person requests the date he
wants to play and whenever possible this happens. Each day of
the competition is made up of 48, 44 and 40 bowlers, multiples
of four, so one in four qualify for the next round. When the
2048 entries are in, the draw is made and in the earlier rounds
bowlers from the same area are kept apart.

The Waterloo is truly the biggest and most popular crown
green competition and consequently the TV coverage has built
from highlights of the final in the Seventies to two full days of
live coverage to take in the last sixteen to the final, which must
place it amongst the major sporting events in the year.

TOP CROWN

On a Sunday in September 1968, a BBC-TV Outside Broadcast
unit established itself at the Waterloo Hotel in Blackpool to
record a crown green bowls tournament to be transmitted on
BBC-2. This was a complete innovation, because it was

the first time a major competition for prize money was played on this famous green on the sabbath. Previously bowling was only allowed for pleasure on Sundays and the organisers strictly adhered to the wishes of the Lord's Day Observance Society by not charging an admission fee. Also, no betting was allowed. Nevertheless there was a full house and the only drawback to the day from the television point of view was that it ended in near darkness.

The series was called the BBC Crown Green Masters Singles and the Producer was Ray Lakeland, Senior Sports Producer in Manchester. The commentators were Harold Webb, the political and industrial correspondent for BBC-TV North, and George Woodcock, the TUC General Secretary, both keen bowlers. It was the first time crown green bowling had been presented on television and sixteen top bowlers were invited to take part. The leading pair were the inimitable Billy Dawber and a young potential star called Noel Burrows. The competition was won by the favourite Dawber, who beat Dick Meyrick 21–12 in the final.

It was an instant success, and the BBC immediately commissioned another series for the following year. It was a personal success for Ray Lakeland and the crown green fraternity were overwhelmed at this breakthrough into what they called 'the big time'.

The following year Ray decided to sharpen up the presentation and also bring in a new commentator to replace Harold Webb, who was unavailable. Harry Rigby had assisted Harold in the first series, and was an acknowledged expert on the game. Harry virtually became a star overnight with his personalised style and colloquial Stockport phraseology. So Ray Lakeland, who pioneered Rugby League on television and discovered Eddie Waring, had found another TV natural. That 1969 competition was won by one of the great characters of modern-day crown green, Roy Armson, who easily beat Larry Greene 21–5.

A change at the top of BBC-2 during 1970–2 meant a break in the progress of crown green bowling on television and the next series was not actually transmitted until 1972. Once again there was a major change in personnel, but Harry Rigby had now become the number one commentator. Another up-and-coming TV personality was teamed with Harry, the jovial Stuart Hall, who made an instant impact on TV viewers – particularly the ladies!

During this period an experimental series had been made for television. The players consisted of four 'panel' bowlers – professional players – who competed in a 'round robin' tournament: Geoff Wardle, Roy Armson, Jack Everitt and Dennis Mercer. The idea was to brighten up the crown green game for television and specially coloured bowls were made. Unfortunately the idea didn't work very well and consequently, in 1973, the TV series reverted back to what was then the standard amateur game. That 1972 series was won by the great Dennis Mercer, who defeated the 1970 Waterloo champion Jack Everitt in the final 15–9. What did stick from the experimental competition was the use of the coloured bowls. So in 1973 the *Top Crown* programme was introduced with the contestants from the quarter-final stages to the grand final – the televised part of the tournament – playing with blue, yellow, red and black sets of bowls.

Eddie Elson had taken over as Secretary of the British Crown Green Amateur Association in 1972, so he had the job of organising this new competition with the coloured bowls. The players were perplexed and unhappy at this, as they had always played with their own bowls and literally took them to bed with them at night so as not to lose sight of them. They also argued that Tony Jacklin wouldn't be asked to play with coloured clubs and golf balls or snooker players with coloured cues. Another problem arose. As the coloured bowls were only being used from the quarter-final stages onwards, the players complained that they couldn't really play with their own bowls in the preliminary stages and suddenly change to the coloured ones, which they had never had in their hands before. They might be too heavy, too big, etc. Poor Eddie had the task of sorting this out. Eventually he told the players that it was an invitation tournament and if they didn't want to take part in it, there would be no difficulty in finding players who did!

So the tournament went ahead in 1973, the year the word 'amateur' was taken out of the British Crown Green title. The significance of this was that the first official prize money was played for in *Top Crown*, with the top prize worth £400. Even the first-round losers received £12 and 10 shillings – which paid for a couple of days in Blackpool!

When the 1973 competition reached the quarter-final stages, coloured bowls were allocated to the players who had won through from the earlier rounds. Again there was an uproar – each player complaining about each pair of bowls. The red ones were too heavy, the yellow were too light, the blue bowls were so weak they virtually had no bias at all. Only the black ones were accepted. In fact, the makers of the coloured bowls, Clare's of Liverpool, had checked and double-checked and all the bowls were exactly the same: evenly matched. Of course, it was all psychological and the bowlers had convinced themselves that they were different.

Eventually this first traumatic series was won by Brian Duncan, 'the panel bowler', which still caused concern to some of the established amateur players. He defeated Dennis Mercer 21–6 in the final and Dennis blamed his poor performance on the blue coloured bowls. It was to be the first of three victories for Brian in the *Top Crown* Singles Competition, and he was firmly establishing himself as the number one crown green bowler.

1974 saw the addition of coloured clothing to go with the bowls and once again there were protests. The anoraks were made of nylon and the players had to wear coloured peak caps. Of course, the anoraks brought on perspiration, and the peak caps obstructed the players' view when they bent down to bowl, all preventing them from playing their best! The favourite, Brian Duncan, retained his title, defeating the colourful Freddie Hulme from Stockport 21–15 and once more reaffirming his number one position.

Being a totally BBC-sponsored event, *Top Crown* was used as a guinea pig for televised bowling; constantly trying out new ideas to enhance the presentation. In 1975, another innovation joined the coloured bowls and clothing: the white jack. This was because there were still a large number of black and white television sets at that time and viewers had complained that they couldn't easily differentiate between the bowls and the jack. The format was still the same – 16 invited players, including the previous year's winner and eight county representatives. The first prize had increased to £500, with a total prize money of £1150 – one of the biggest in the game. Stuart Hall left the programme and Manchester-born Tony Gubba teamed up with Harry Rigby to fill the gap in the commentary team.

At this time there were some diehards of the amateur game who were unhappy because there were still two sets of rules, one set for the Panel at the Waterloo and another for the British Crown Green Association. The referees had a difficult time because the Waterloo rules allowed 'stamping' close to the bowl and running alongside. The British Crown Green rules didn't allow 'stamping' and, in fact, players were not allowed within three metres of the running bowl. These people complained about the likes of Brian Duncan running and stamping and the fact that they thought the British Crown Green were prostituting the sport for the sake of television with the use of coloured bowls and clothing. However, the association decided that television was the most important vehicle to get the sport across to the country and so they worked alongside the television requirements despite the protests.

It was in 1975 that Brian Duncan was on for a 'three in a row' and once again made it to the final. His opponent was the second favourite, Dennis Mercer, who, after his defeat by Duncan in 1973, predicted he would win *Top Crown* and beat him in the process. During the final, Dennis was constantly topping up his favourite pipe – getting it to blow out victory signals as he stormed home to a 21–16 victory to deny Duncan a fabulous hat-trick and also enhance his reputation as a fortune-teller.

Brian Duncan and Dennis Mercer dominated the *Top Crown* competition between 1972 and 1979 – Duncan winning the title three times and losing the final once and Mercer with two titles and two runner-up prizes. The two barren years for them were 1976 and 1978, when Tony Poole from the Midlands made his impact on the crown green scene in the north and won the title in 1976. It was this year that actor and writer Colin Welland came on the scene as co-commentator with Harry Rigby. Born in the Wigan area he had been brought up on crown green bowling and therefore settled in to the job extremely well. He was well-liked by the viewers and public, working alongside Harry in both *Top Crown* and the Waterloo until 1979, when his writing really took off and his spare time was severely limited.

In 1977 another Midlands bowler, Roy Price, created a sensation when he defeated Brian Duncan in the semi-final and then 'dumped' Dennis Mercer 21–16 in the final. Gene Bardon and Roy Nicholson – both Yorkshiremen – battled out the 1978 final, Bardon winning an extremely close match 21–19.

The 1979 *Top Crown* tournament was to be the last singles competition, as it was felt it wasn't getting the public or viewer support it deserved, and 1980 saw the first BBC-TV *Top Crown* Pairs Invitation Tournament. It was a two-bowl player competition, and, with the extra four bowls, it was hoped there would be more green drama. In the first pairs competition it was also decided not to use the coloured bowls any more, which pleased most of the bowlers. This was primarily because there were now 40 bowlers taking part – 16 invited pairs from the counties and four pairs (including the holders) invited by the BBC – the champions being seeded through to the quarter-finals. The contestants were kitted out in coloured sweaters and the same coloured stickers were put on to the bowls for easier identification by the viewing public. Richard Duckenfield, himself a member of the St Helens Bowling Club, now joined Harry Rigby in the commentary box and the first pairs competition in any form of bowling on television was born.

The 1980 series was eventually won by Noel Burrows, partnered by Mike Leach from Blackpool. They beat Terry Turner and Keith Widdowson in the final 21–16. Mike Leach was potentially an exciting player for television because of his unusually jerky delivery, and in fact he won the British Crown Green title in 1984. Unfortunately his delivery began to cause problems and he has played little competitive bowls since 1985.

1981 and 1982 were both 'Wars of the Roses', with Duncan and his regular pairs partner Norman Fletcher being firm favourites both years. Gene Bardon and Roy Nicholson, however, ignored the reputation of the Lancashire pair and hammered them 21–13 in the 1981 final. At this time, the BBC were still having trouble with long matches, so in 1982 yet again experimented with playing 15 up. Duncan and Fletcher duly reached the final and another Yorkshire pair, Allan Thompson and Robert Hitchen, had the task of stopping them. This match will go into the history books as one of the most controversial finals in televised crown green. The score was 14–13 to the Yorkshiremen at the beginning of the penultimate end, but Duncan and Fletcher had already put one closest and Norman Fletcher bowled for the title. It was a winner all the way, but referee Barry Cotterill stunned the Waterloo crowd into silence by removing Fletcher's bowl – having ruled that he got too close to the bowl and therefore 'stamped' it in. You may remember the reference to the confusion of British Crown and Waterloo rules earlier in this chapter and of course Duncan and Fletcher, particularly, constantly played to the Waterloo rules. *Top Crown* was played to BCGBA rules and it wasn't until after Jack Leigh took over the Waterloo in 1982 that a standard set of rules was negotiated for the Waterloo as well as other events organised by the British Crown.

The ensuing pandemonium saw Duncan and Fletcher almost on the point of leaving the green, but they carried on to lose 15–14 and the inscrutable Thompson and Hitchen were *Top Crown* champions 1982. It's a story that has been told by people with slightly different points of view. British Secretary Eddie Elson went on television and defended Barry Cotterill's action – it was a brave decision and one that perhaps not every referee would have been prepared to take. BCGBA Rule 22 stated a player must not approach nearer than one metre to a running bowl, nor follow it up in such a manner as to obstruct the view of his opponent. He must not endeavour to accelerate or impede its progress. If he offends, the bowl shall be taken out of play and in case of further infringement, his bowls shall be taken off the green and the game shall be awarded to his opponent and the defaulter's score at that point to count! Obviously referee Cotterill had deemed Fletcher guilty of breaking the law and applied Rule 22, and the controversial final was dubbed as the most expensive stamp since the 'Penny Black'!

In 1984, for the first time, *Top Crown* wasn't played at the Waterloo Hotel. This decision was made for two reasons. There had been constant lobbying over the past few years from other bowling clubs to stage this prestigious event, and also the public attending the event looked lost in such a vast stadium. It was therefore played at the Mitchell and Butlers Sports Club in Birmingham – a beautiful setting for the star Manchester pair of Eddie Hulbert and Tommy Johnstone to beat the 1983 champions, Ken Strutt and Dave Blackburn, 21–15 in the final.

In 1985 the event had become so popular with the bowlers, not least for the £2000 first prize, that they all wanted to take part: 64 starters were entered – 16 pairs from the counties and 16 pairs invited by the BBC, with no seeds. We decided to keep on the idea of changing venues, despite a poor crowd at Birmingham, and we moved to the Manchester GEC Club.

Top Crown has always been the 'guinea-pig' competition for crown green bowling, and 1986 saw another innovation. This was to be a major leap forward in the history of the game as four ladies' pairs were invited to compete on equal terms with the men. The tournament was played at the Pilkington Sports Club in St Helens and, on a large, fast green, the ladies had their work cut out. However two ladies' pairs reached the quarter-finals, and in the semi-finals the last pair, Karen Galvin and Mary Farmer, fell to the favourites Brian Duncan and Norman

Fletcher, who eventually went on to win the title in a tight, hard game 21–19 against the 1984 winners Eddie Hulbert and Tommy Johnstone.

Top Crown semi-finalists 1986. l-r: Norman Fletcher, Brian Duncan, Karen Galvin and Mary Farmer

CHAPTER 8

STARS OF THE CROWN GAME

KEITH PHILLIPS

BRIAN DUNCAN

Brian Duncan, Top Crown Trophy Singles Winner 1974

Brian, aged 43, is a bowls manufacturer based in Preston. A member of the Railway Hotel at Lostock and also Baxi of Leyland Bowling Clubs, he has played many times for Lancashire and is the winner of countless competitions, notably the Waterloo in 1979 and 1986, retaining the Blackpool Talbot in 1974, the Bass Masters in 1985 and the Top Crown Pairs in 1986. Brian has never won the 'All England'; the nearest he came was in 1985 when he was beaten in the final. In 1986, he won seven top competitions.

Brian Duncan is the undisputed number one of the crown green game and has been since 1964. He started playing with his father at an early age and at 18 played for Lancashire. By 21 he had won the Lancashire Merit and throughout his career has won almost every major competition in the game. He has a distinctive way of playing the crown game. He is very quick, tries to force the pace, and runs after nearly every bowl he delivers. He prefers to play corner to corner and on slow-running greens. He has played on so many greens he knows most of them by heart. He picks the marks where he feels he can beat his opponent and rarely varies from his selected area. Many players have different ideas how to beat him, but the favourite theme is to slow him down and get him away from his favourite marks. If it's a fast green, by planting your bowls two feet or a yard off the jack, you stand a chance because Brian is never short and could go through the gap. If your bowls are too close, he'll knock them out.

He's an obvious choice to be invited into the mixed flat indoor competitions, but has really yet to find his feet. Should he in future spend more time learning the flat game, he should be amongst the top indoor players. His problem will be adjusting from his speed and skill at putting the bowl to the jack to the slower-paced flat game, which brings in more tactics and strategy than the crown game.

Brian is also a very successful pairs player, being a finalist in 1981 and 1982 in the BBC-2 Top Crown Pairs and eventually becoming champion in 1986. On all these occasions he was partnered by Norman Fletcher.

NOEL BURROWS

Noel Burrows, aged 43, is a general manager at Bowlers club in Trafford Park, and plays for the Sale Excelsior Club in Manchester. Major tournament wins include the BCGBA Merit in 1976, John Player (Embassy) Champion of Champions in 1978, the John Player (Embassy) in 1980, the Bass Masters in 1982 and the Granada Superbowl (flat) Championship in 1985.

Noel is probably the country's best-known bowler in the crown code due to his success in both his own crown tournaments and indoor flat TV competitions. He started bowling at the age of four, playing with his grandfather and father on the bowling green beside the Red Lion Hotel at

Noel Burrows – leading bowler in both flat and crown codes

Withington, Manchester. Both men were landlord in their time and Noel eventually became host himself in later years.

Noel didn't take up competitive bowling until he was just turned twenty, and remembers his first major tournament – the William Husband at Hyde. Having got to the semi-finals, he put a £1 bet on himself with a well-known bookie called 'Brownie', who gave him odds of 3–1. He won the tournament, was given £3 by Brownie, and was just about to leave when a friend said, 'Have you got your stake money back?' He went back to the bookie who apologised and gave him his £1 stake. His first lesson in the world of competitive bowling!

In the same year Noel drew Vernon Lee in the famous Warrington Charities Competition. He went to watch Vernon play in a 'Panel' game to learn about his opponent, which surprised the more experienced bowlers, and consequently, to everyone's astonishment, beat him.

Later he won the News of the World and, in 1968, the Lancashire Merit – which his father had won in 1959. They were only the second father and son in history to win, the others being Bill Parr Senior and Junior from St Helens. In 1970 he reached the last sixteen of the Waterloo, but was beaten by the eventual winner, Jack Everitt, and in 1971 got to the last sixteen again, only to be beaten by the great Billy Dawber.

Noel was beginning to reach peak form and in 1972 he achieved the dream of crown bowlers and reached the final of the Waterloo, eventually winning the competition in front of a proud father applauding from the stands.

In 1973 he reached the final of the old Talbot Handicap, only to lose 21–17, not quite achieving the crowning ambition of bowlers in those days – to do the double, the Talbot and Waterloo. Unfortunately the Talbot was abandoned after 1975.

Noel was the pioneer of the entry into the flat game for crown green bowlers. He was invited to enter the John Player Classic, a mixed competition especially set up for BBC-TV's *Grandstand*, which included flat, crown, ladies and federation players. He finished fifth overall, but had the distinction of beating the famous Norma Shaw in the qualifying rounds. David Bryant was another of his victims – 15–2 in an exhibition match during this event. Noel has the distinction of being the only crown bowler to win a flat tournament, beating David Bryant in the final of the 1985 Superbowl 7–6, 7–5, 0–7, 7–6. In fact, he has beaten David three times out of the four times they have met.

Noel still has ambitions to be top in crown and flat, but his ultimate ambition is to win the World Indoor Singles Title and then visit the world playing for England.

ROY ARMSON

Roy Armson, aged 58, is an engineering representative. He plays for the Sale Excelsior Club in Manchester and has played for the three counties of Greater Manchester, Lancashire and Cheshire, making a total of 99 county appearances. Major tournament wins include the Greenall Whitley County Classic, Carr Mill in 1987, the British Parks, the Isle of Man, the News of the World and the BBC Masters.

Roy is one of the man-made bowlers, who started playing around 1960. He says he had no natural flair for the game and taught himself how to play. However he lives bowls and is a

Roy Armson in action during Top Crown

great student of the game. It is said that if Roy Armson is not in a competition, it's not worth playing in, as he enters nearly every tournament on the circuit. You can immediately recognise Roy by his tartan cap, and he has the odd characteristic of leaning against the way the bowl is travelling, rather than the natural instinct to lean towards the jack. Another characteristic is that he appears to be nervous when he's about to deliver and has been known to prepare to bowl three or four times before actually releasing the bowl. He's a great tactician and always has a plan, for he does his homework on his opponents, and he is a fount of knowledge on greens and equipment at different clubs.

Roy won his first major competition in 1967 – the St Andrews at Burnley – and then the News of the World at Preston in 1969. That same year he won the Top Crown Singles Championship, but it was to be his last important win for some considerable time. It is remarkable that Roy has won hundreds of smaller competitions, but the prestige and television tournaments seem to elude him. He was in nineteen finals one season – won ten and lost nine – but none were well-known. He has never won the Waterloo or the British Crown Green Merit and it was not until 1986 that he won another major title. It had been suggested by some that when the pressure was on, he didn't seem to be able to make it, but when he won the Greenall Whitley County Classic in 1986 he actually came back from 12–19 down to win the title. So much for 'no bottle'!

His choice of pairs partner seems to depend on which side of Bolton the competition is taking place. If it's to the west he plays with Norman Heslop and if it's to the east, with Noel Burrows. He started playing with Noel in 1975, when they won the Bass Olympia, and they have stayed together since. Noel tells a story illustrating how meticulous Roy is when playing bowls. In 1984 the pair had reached the last eight of the Whitbread pairs at Clough Hotel, Blackley, Manchester. They won their match comfortably, but Roy wasn't satisfied with his bowls. He changed for another set in the semi-finals, which they again won comfortably, but he still wasn't satisfied and changed his bowls for the final. They also won the championship, but Roy had actually used three different sets of bowls from the quarter-finals to the final.

His wife Doris also plays, and is now one of the top lady bowlers, having won many competitions – including the Ladies' Waterloo. Doris also helps Roy with his 'hobby' as a bookie – when he's knocked out of his competitions.

TONY POOLE

Tony Poole, aged 45, is a trophy and bowls retailer. He plays for the Castlefields Club in Shrewsbury, and has been a prolific winner over the years. Playing for Shropshire over 100 times, he won the 'All England' in 1971 and was the losing finalist in 1974. He was BBC Masters and Hepworth Daily Express winner in 1976, Champion of Champions winner in both 1976 and 1984, and the Shropshire Champion on three occasions. In addition, he has won many other competitions including events on the flat and the GEC at Stafford in 1985.

A very popular player in the crown game, Tony first came to prominence when he won the British Crown Green Merit in 1971 at the age of 30. He led the way for Midland bowlers to take a more professional attitude to the game when the British

Tony Poole – top Midlands Crown Green competitor

Crown Green Association dropped the word amateur from its title and became open in 1973, entering the more prestigious competitions in the north – with richer pickings – and winning on many occasions. It wasn't long before many other previously sceptical bowlers followed.

Tony was a true pioneer for the Midlands. He was also one of the first crown green bowlers to be involved in the new successful indoor flat competitions. One of the first times he played flat was in a special television competition involving four flat and four crown green bowlers. The players spent three days in Cardiff playing flat and, the following week, three days playing crown in Rhyl. The indoor game really appealed to Tony and from then on there was no stopping him.

His favourite length on a crown green is about 25–30 yards, which is complementary to the length in indoor flat rinks, and this obviously suits him for both codes. Although he has been invited to play in many indoor television competitions, he has the disadvantage of not having an indoor rink to play or practise on within any reasonable distance, a pity because Tony is a thinking player, a great tactician, and wants to learn to play the indoor game the true flat way and not with any crown tendencies.

He recently played in a television special with Noel Burrows – another convert to the flat game – against David Bryant and Mal Hughes, at a venue near Birmingham which has both a flat and a crown rink. They played flat in the morning and crown in the afternoon and both matches ended very close at 21–19. Perhaps this may lead to more playing of mixed codes in the future. Tony Poole was also the first Midlands bowler to win the Top Crown Singles tournament, beating Norman Dawkes 21–12 in the final of 1976.

CHAPTER 9

THE LADIES' GAME
KEITH PHILLIPS

Norma Shaw during the 1985 British Isles Championship

In writing a book about bowling one cannot ignore the contribution that ladies have made to the game. I hope that the ladies of the flat green game will forgive me for not devoting many words to their game in this book. The reason is relatively simple. The book is based around televised tournaments, and generally speaking the ladies' flat game is not really involved in televised events. That is of course, up to the present. Conversely, lady crown green bowlers have made inroads into the men's tournaments both indoors and out, particularly in televised events and there is a possibility that some coverage will be given to the Ladies' Waterloo tournament in the near future.

Ladies' bowls can be traced back as far as the 14th century, and in May 1661 Samuel Pepys entered in his diary, 'Today very merry and played at bowls with our wives.' It was not, however, until the early 1900s that the numbers of ladies playing grew to any great proportion. One of the oldest ladies' bowling leagues is in Manchester, which was formed on 2 October 1918. At that time matches were cancelled at the sight of rain, whereas nowadays they play in the worst of conditions, wearing so much clothing that they are often not recognisable as the fairer sex!

In the Wirral the ladies had to belong to the co-op before they were allowed to play in their local league, and during the great wars the ladies working in munitions factories organised competitions. They charged one shilling as an entry fee and the contributions went to wartime charities. They actually were allowed to play on a selected men's green, but not when the men were playing.

During this time the ladies really only played for fun. The British Parks Merit (organised by the men) seems to be the earliest ladies' open handicap on record and was won in 1932 by Mrs McAlister of Lancashire. Apart from a break during the war years and one from 1956 to 1975 – due to lack of interest and support – this handicap has been going from strength to strength. The Parks Secretary, Ray Angus, anticipates a record number of 2000 entries in 1987, with preliminary rounds being played on own greens and the final 64 players coming to Cleckheaton in Yorkshire. Pat Davies of Wirral, who won the title in 1981, 1985 and 1986, is on for a hat trick. She has already set a record that will be a challenge to all lady bowlers and will take some beating.

Another popular tournament is the Ladies' Open at New Brighton, which started in 1935 and in 1986 attracted over 500 entries. In 1937, a Mr Hartley of Preston formed a Manchester/Liverpool/Fylde and Preston combination known as the Lancashire County Ladies Association; one of the very few men who had the ladies' interests at heart.

The Second World War intervened and, apart from the New Brighton competition, only local leagues were prominent. During the war the bowling carried on, but the matches were often interrupted by air raids. The ruling then was that all cards were scrapped and the matches were abandoned and had to be played from the beginning again. A large number of matches took a few weeks to complete. At the present time, if a match has to be interrupted, the bowls are marked and the game carries on from where it stopped.

It has often been remarked that ladies' prizes have consisted only of tea pots and pillowcases, but the prizes do seem to have reflected the demands of the era. Hence, during the war, the prizes consisted of war savings stamps, and when there was a coal shortage, one lady player remembers winning half a bag of coal and being the envy of all. This was for an entry fee of 1s 3d, including greenage! Now, of course, in 1987, most handicaps are for money. The most lucrative event is the Greenall Whitley Ladies' Waterloo, in which over 1200 play off on the famous green for a first prize of £1000. Maureen Bresnan of the Wirral won this in 1986 and the total prize money was £4320.

The first Ladies' Waterloo was organised by Mary Ashcroft, after watching her husband play in the men's competition in 1975. She asked the late Tom Bradley, who was running the Waterloo at that time, 'Why can't ladies have a Waterloo Handicap?' Tom's reply was anything but positive, but Mary didn't back down and continued to pressure Tom whenever she could. Eventually he could take no more and said to Mary, 'If you organise the event yourself, you can have your own tournament.'

So in 1977 the first Ladies' Waterloo got under way with 256 entrants, paying £1 each to play, for a first prize of £100. To many people's surprise, 500 spectators turned up to watch and Tom was most impressed. So the next year he allowed an increase in starters – in fact double the first year, to 512. The figure stayed at this for a while, as dates for the ladies were hard to fix due to the increase in men's competitions at the Waterloo Hotel. It wasn't until Jack Leigh came along in the early Seventies that the tournament grew again. He decided to give the ladies two full weeks for their handicap and therefore the chance to increase their entrants to 1000. So, since 1977, the number of entries has increased from 256 to 1000, the entrance fee from £1 to £3.50 and the first prize from £100 to £1000. This is quite an achievement since the First World War, as most ladies have only played for their own enjoyment until the last few years.

Suddenly ladies' crown green began to take off; more and more competitions with good prize money from more-than-interested sponsors. The bowls makers Thos. Taylor, for instance, sponsored a Ladies' Champion of Champions Tournament last year, which was tremendously successful, and of course Superbowl invites lady crown green bowlers to compete against the men in their indoor flat competition. As you may have read in an earlier chapter, the BBC invited four ladies' pairs to compete on equal terms with the males for the

Top Crown trophy last year for the first time, and two of the pairs made it to the quarter-finals and one to the semi-finals. It seems that as the Ladies' Waterloo has grown, so has the stature of the lady bowlers: more will to win, to be seen on television, to set a higher standard of bowling, and now to travel to enter richer-prized competitions.

A further development since ladies started playing indoor flat has been mixed matches of men and women on level terms playing short mat bowls. This is particularly strong in the north-west of England and is fast becoming a nationwide offshoot of indoor flat bowling. From this, clubs are now being formed with mixed membership and playing in mixed open tournaments. The BCGBA may well be forced to recognise this new development and, in fact, has just agreed to have lady referees for certain competitions – although the ladies themselves would probably be happy to be members of the BCGBA in their own right. A significant move to help the ladies in their objective was also taken in 1987. The Lancashire, Yorkshire, Cheshire and Wirral County Associations joined with the Midlands to form the first British Ladies' County Association.

CHAPTER 10

THE FUTURE OF BOWLS
KEITH PHILLIPS

When the average age of bowlers was much higher than now, the game of fours was the basis of the flat game. Eight bowlers playing two bowls each in a period of five minutes, with a walk of 40 yards to the other end of the green was the civilised way to spend an afternoon of gentle retirement with like-minded colleagues. Younger players, ambitious to succeed at the highest level, are happier playing singles and four-bowl pairs which could lead to team singles in the future.

The game of bowls has progressed in many aspects throughout the years, but this is only the start of a revolution that is about to take place in the game. Television has played a major part in bringing to the public the excitement, skill and entertainment of a bowling tournament, which in turn has brought a surge of interest amongst the younger members of the community.

The last decade has seen 20,000 new members join the English Bowling Association (Outdoor) and 32,000 join the English Indoor Bowling Association, and obviously this doesn't include Scotland, Ireland and Wales. The Women's Association has also increased its membership by almost 50 per cent from 9,000 to 13,000.

So what of the future? The main obstacle, of course, is finance. With so many people wanting to take part in the sport there are not enough clubs to facilitate them. A new purpose-built six-rink indoor centre costs in the region of £250,000. The ones already built have come from groups of enthusiasts with help from the Sports Council and some local authorities. Another trend is towards professional coaches in the newer complexes, such as Tony Allcock's Spanish La Manga club, and Ken Williams at South Tweed Heads in Australia.

As technological production grows and leisure time increases, a demand will be created for full-time coaches and administrators in the game in this country. Surely the time is coming when bowlers will book lessons with their bowls coach as naturally as golfers already do with their club professional.

Will the game follow snooker into Europe and the continents? The future of the sport there will depend on the availability of venues for the portable rink and the publicity for British televised events. Already, outdoor bowls is growing in Spain, France and Italy, and the indoor game is sure to follow. The World Indoor Singles Championship is ready now to have qualifying tournaments staged in countries outside the British Isles which will bring the initial entries into the thousands. Certainly, the promoter of the televised game of bowls has definite sights on these lines for the future.

What of the game itself? Certainly, the televised two-bowl pairs seems to have been a successful innovation indoors, but would it prove successful outdoors? Television coverage is slowly altering the image of the game with many young players coming to the fore. Dress is changing and soon there will be specially designed outfits of different colours for the players. As the game moves into a more professional area, the business attitude is bound to enter increasingly into players' lives with endorsements not only for bowls gear but also for non-bowls products, already started by David Bryant and Tony Allcock. Perhaps in the future there will be a professional players' circus, guaranteed an income from playing in TV tournaments, exhibitions, challenge matches, demonstrations and coaching. Already the seeds are sown for such a possibility by the formation of the Players Associations in England and Scotland.

As a BBC Sports Producer I am very pleased at the contribution television has made to the sport. We have tried to reflect everything that is best in the game and feel it has been streamlined because of our involvement. Indeed, I think television has begun to develop the game for the 20th century and hope it will continue to do so positively.

So the future looks very rosy indeed. Bowls looks set to become fashionable, big business, a major means of entertainment, therapeutic *and* very professional. Indications for the future are difficult to predict, but I believe the sonic measure will become standard practice and the dream of our leading TV commentator David Rhys Jones is certainly possible by the 21st century: a centre-court rink where big competitions could be played outdoors and televised. It would be a single rink, with permanent terracing and a facility for an umbrella cover to guarantee play for television.

Let's hope all our aspirations for the game of bowls are fulfilled in the future, and that it continues to attract an ever-increasing and enthusiastic following.

The crown green game has also begun to change. A profes-sional players association has recently been founded, but the trend certainly is for crown green bowlers to play the indoor flat game, both with ladies and men. Areas where the clubs are not in abundance have seen a rapid rise in the short mat game, particularly in crown green territory, and one of the biggest areas is in the north-west of England.

TOURNAMENT RESULTS

JACK HIGH 1978–86

RESULTS

	Winners	Runners-up
1978	David Bryant 21	Dick Folkins 12
1979	David Bryant 21	David McGill 11
1980	Bill Moseley 21	David McGill 16
1981	Bill Moseley 21	David McGill 14
1982	David Bryant 21	John Snell 12
1983	George Souza 21	David Bryant 19
1984	David Bryant 21	Peter Bellis 16
1985	David Bryant 21	Cecil Bransky 12
1986	David Bryant 21	Ian Dickison 19

WORLD INDOOR SINGLES CHAMPIONSHIP 1979–87

RESULTS

	Winners	Runners-up
1979	David Bryant 21	Jim Donnelly 14
1980	David Bryant 21	Philip Chok 15
1981	David Bryant 21	John Thomas 18
1982	John Watson 21	Jim Baker 13
1983	Bob Sutherland 21	Burnie Gill 10
1984	Jim Baker 21	Nigel Smith 18
1985	Terry Sullivan 21	Cecil Bransky 18
1986	Tony Allcock 21	Phil Skoglund 15
1987	Tony Allcock 5	David Bryant 4*

THE WATERLOO 1907–86

	Winners	Runners-up
1907	Jas Rothwell West Leigh	T. Richardson South Shore
1908	Geo. Beatty Burnley	James Southern Darwen
1909	Tom Meadows West Leigh	W. H. Andrews Stalybridge
1910	No Handicap	
1911	John Peace Huddersfield	F. Walmsley Blackburn
1912	T. Lowe Westhoughton	C. Farrington Howe Bridge

1913	Gerard Hart	R. Hart
	Blackrod	Blackrod
1914	John Rothwell	F. Percival
	Atherton	Wilmslow
1915	W. Fairhurst	Walter Simms
	Standish	Aspull
1916	J. Parkinson	E. Hall
	Oldham	Platt Bridge
1917	G. Barnes	H. Hemingway
	Westhoughton	Burnley
1918	W. Simms	J. Pimblett
	Aspull	Pemberton
1919	Len Moss	T. Richardson
	Denton	South Shore
1920	E. Whiteside	D. Brown
	Lytham	Lostock Hall
1921	J. Bagot	Walter Guest
	South Shore	Bury
1922	W. A. Smith	Geo. Barnes
	Old Trafford	Westhoughton
1923	J. Martin	Geo. Barnes
	Westhoughton	Westhoughton
1924	Rowland Hill	R. Banks
	Brynn	Bolton
1925	Jack Cox	T. Whittle
	Blackpool	Ashton-in-Makerfield
1926	T. Roscoe	T. Cornwell
	Blackpool	Chorley
1927	H. Waddecar	Seth Mason
	Midge Hall	Blackrod
1928	T. Whittle	J. Meadows
	Ashton-in-Makerfield	South Shore
1929	Chas. Halpin	J. Hart
	Blackpool	Hollinwood
1930	J. Chadwick	W. Park
	Westhoughton	Preston
1931	A. Gleave	W. Grace
	Warrington	Blackpool
1932	T. E. Booth	T. Davies
	West Didsbury	Atherton
1933	A. Ogden	R. Thomas
	Failsworth	Hindley
1934	W. Derbyshire	W. Hargreaves
	Burnley	Blackburn
1935	C. Roberts	R. Thomas
	Fearnhead	Hindley
1936	H. Yates	F. Wolstencroft
	Preston	North Shore
1937	A. King	T. Suttie
	Windermere	Blackburn
1938	J. W. Whitter	D. Jacks
	Standish	Kearsley

1939	Abandoned	
1940	H. Holden	J. Swithenbank
	Blackpool	Blackpool
1941	W. J. Wilcock	W. Finch
	St Helens	Blackpool
1942	T. Bimson	J. Ormond
	Hardhorn	Blackpool
1943	S. Ivell	J. Stevenson
	Little Hulton	Blackpool
1944	T. Tinker	T. Richardson
	Huddersfield	Blackpool
1945	W. Grace	D. Ayrton
	Blackpool	Blackpool
1946	C. Parkinson	T. Bimson
	Pemberton	Hardhorn
1947	W. Dalton	R. Robinson
	Fleetwood	Preston
1948	A. E. Ringrose	W. Derbyshire
	Bradford	Newtown
1949	J. Egan	J. Lawton
	Birkdale	Lancaster
1950	H. Finch	W. Green
	Blackpool	Blackrod
1951	J. Waterhouse	T. Bimson
	Middleton	Hardhorn
1952	L. Thompson	W. Worthington
	St Helens	Droylsden
1953	B. Kelly	H. Taberner
	Hyde	Altrincham
1954	B. Kelly	A. Holden
	Hyde	Fulwood
1955	J. Heyes	G. Bromley
	Aspull	Blackpool
1956	J. Sumner	H. Pennington
	Blackpool	Whiston
1957	W. Lacy	T. Bimson
	Wigan	St Anne's
1958	F. Salisbury	W. Carter
	Preston	Rainhill
1959	W. Dawber	H. Wallwork
	Wrightington	Pendlebury
1960	H. Bury	J. Featherstone
	Blackpool	Leigh
1961	J. Featherstone	C. Taylor
	Leigh	Blackpool
1962	J. Collier	Tom Mayor
	Pendleton	Bolton
1963	T. Mayor	D. Hogarth
	Bolton	Lytham
1964	W. B. Heinkey	L. Taylor
	Birmingham	Swinton
1965	J. Pepper	A. Wood
	Salford	Broughton

1966	R. Collier	F. Mountford
	Little Hulton	Rochdale
1967	Eric Ashton	D. Kirkham
	Towyn	Chorlton-cum-Hardy
1968	Billy Bennett	A. Thompson
	Warrington	Carleton
1969	G. T. Underwood	C. E. Jackson
	Blackpool	Andsell
1970	Jack Everitt	A. Howarth
	Willenhall	Royton
1971	J. Bradbury	S. V. Ellis
	Romiley	Blackpool
1972	N. Burrows	W. Brindle
	Withington	Bolton
1973	A. Murray	J. Hadfield
	Partington	Preston
1974	W. Houghton	S. V. Ellis
	Freckleton	Blackpool
1975	J. Collen	S. A. Rogers
	Bury	Davyhulme
1976	K. Illingworth	S. Buckley
	Blackpool	Chadderton
1977	L. Barrett	L. Gilfedder
	Whitefield	Warrington
1978	A. Murray	W. H. Smith
	Partington	Wirral
1979	B. Duncan	A. Broadhurst
	Leigh	Aspull
1980	V. Lee	G. Vernon
	Blackpool	Winsford
1981	R. Nicholson	B. Prolze
	Brighouse	Altrincham
1982	D. Mercer	K. Strutt
	Stockport	Oldham
1983	S. Frith	B. Henstead
	Weaverham	Wigan
1984	S. Ellis	J. Lees
	Kirkham	Walton-le-Dale
1985	T. Johnstone	A. Thompson
	Manchester	Mirfield
1986	B. Duncan	J. Sykes
	Leigh	Mirfield

TOP CROWN 1968–86

BBC Crown Green Masters

	Winners	*Runners-up*
1968	W. Dawber 21	Dick Meyrick 12
1969	Roy Armson 21	Larry Greene 5
1970	No Competition	
1971	No Competition	
1972	Dennis Mercer 15	Jack Everitt 9

Top Crown

Winners	Runners-up
1973 Brian Duncan 21	Dennis Mercer 6
1974 Brian Duncan 21	Fred Hulme 15
1975 Dennis Mercer 21	Brian Duncan 16
1976 Tony Poole 21	Norman Dawkes 12
1977 Roy Price 21	Dennis Mercer 16
1978 Gene Bardon 21	Roy Nicholson 19
1979 Brian Duncan 21	Noel Burrows 10

Top Crown – Pairs Tournament

Winners	Runners-up
1980 Noel Burrows and Mike Leach 21	Terry Turner and Keith Widdowson 16
1981 Gene Bardon and Roy Nicholson 21	Brian Duncan and Norman Fletcher 13
1982 Allan Thompson and Robert Hitchen 15	Brian Duncan and Norman Fletcher 14
1983 Ken Strutt and David Blackburn 15	Robert Hitchen and Allan Thompson 11
1984 Eddie Hulbert and Tommy Johnstone 21	Ken Strutt and David Blackburn 15
1985 Robert Hitchen and Roy Nicholson 21	Frank Kitchen and Michael Eccles 17
1986 Brian Duncan and Norman Fletcher 21	Tommy Johnstone and Eddie Hulbert 19

GLOSSARY

FLAT GREEN

Bias: That which is inbuilt into the bowl, which causes the bowl to travel in a curve.

Forehand: When for the right-handed player the bowl is delivered so that the curve of the bowl is from right to left towards its objective.

Backhand: When for the right-handed player the bowl is delivered so that the curve of the bowl is from left to right towards its objective.

Shoulder of the Green: That point on the green where the bowl begins to curve inwards towards its objective.

Foot Fault: The rear foot must be on or above the mat at the moment of delivery, and if it is not, then the player could incur a penalty.

The Mat: A bowler must make his delivery from the mat (the size of the mat is 24in by 14in).

Long Jack: The greatest distance allowed from the front edge of the mat to the jack.

Short Jack: The shortest distance allowed from the front edge of the mat to the jack.

Ditch: The green is surrounded by a depression whose edge marks the boundary of the playing surface. Measurements of the ditch need to conform to the laws of the game.

Rink: A rectangular area of the green not more than 19ft or less than 18ft wide on which play takes place.

String: Normally a green 'string' drawn tightly along the green to define the boundaries of the rink.

Jack or Kitty: The white ball towards which play is directed.

Push and Rest: The bowling of a bowl of sufficient pace or weight that it pushes a bowl from its position so that that position is taken by the last bowl delivered.

Trail the Jack: A bowl played in order to move the jack to another position on the rink.

Block or Stopper: A wood delivered with enough pace to stop short of the objective, in the hope that it will prevent an opponent being able to play a certain shot.

Fire or Drive: There are various reasons for such a shot, but it is a shot where the bowl is delivered at a very fast pace.

Toucher: A bowl which during its course has touched the jack.

Toucher in the Ditch: A toucher as above which has fallen into the ditch shall be a 'live' wood, but not if it has come to rest outside the confines of the rink.

The Shot: The bowl that finishes nearest to the jack at any stage of play.

The Head: The jack and as many bowls as have been played at any stage of any end. Bowls in the head may be on the rink or in the ditch.

Dead Wood or Bowl: A bowl which comes to rest in the ditch, or is knocked into the ditch and is not a toucher. Or a bowl that comes to rest outside the confines of the rink, either in its course or by being knocked there.

Live Bowl/Wood: Any bowl that comes to rest within the confines of the rink and allowing for conditions as laid down by the laws of the game. Or any toucher in the ditch.

Dead End: An end which is considered not to have been played and for which no score is recorded. It can happen as a result of the jack being driven out of the confines of the playing area.

A Plant Shot: Where a player bowls his wood to strike other woods which could be in line, and thus gain his objective.

The Marker: A person who in a game of singles undertakes to see the game played according to the rules, will mark all touchers, centre the jack and measure as well as keeping the score.

CROWN GREEN

Cobbing: Northern term used to describe a certain type of delivery used when the green is waterlogged. Bowl is thrown over puddles. Not elegant but effective.

Blocker: Bowl bowled short of a length so as to impede line from footer to jack or short bowl.

Footer: Circular rubber/plastic disc from which delivery of jack and bowls must be made.

Length Bowl: Bowl has finished its traction and is level with the length of the jack.

No Weight: Term used to indicate that player is bowling consistently long or short of the jack.

Stamping: Illegal use of feet stamping near to running bowl to accelerate or promote greater distance.

Shunting: When opponent has bowled short, bowling up the same line/land as opponent's bowl to push his bowl nearer the jack.

PICTURE ACKNOWLEDGEMENTS

Front cover Bob Thomas Sports Photography; page 11 David Rhys Jones; page 15 City of Plymouth Museums & Art Gallery; page 18 BBC Hulton Picture Library; pages 19, 21, 23, 28, 34 (all), 35 (all), 36 (both), 37 (both), 44 & 53 Duncan Cubitt; pages 55 & 57 Eric Whitehead; page 59 Duncan Cubitt; page 61 Eric Whitehead; page 64 Bob Thomas Sports Photography; page 69 Aberdeen Evening Express; pages 72, 74, 76, 79 (both) & 80 Duncan Cubitt; page 86 Eddie Elson; page 91 Greenall Whitley Waterloo Bowling; page 92 BBC; pages 93, 94, 95 & 96 Greenall Whitley Waterloo Bowling; pages 105, 106, 108 & 110 BBC; page 112 Tony Poole; page 114 Duncan Cubitt; back cover BBC.